1988

Performing Your Best

Tom Kubistant, EdD

Performance and Productivity Specialists
Reno, NV

Life Enhancement Publications
Champaign, Illinois

Library of Congress Cataloging-in-Publication Data

Kubistant, Tom, 1950-
   Performing your best.

   Bibliography: p.
   Includes index.
   1. Success. 2. Entertainers—Conduct of life.
I. Title

BJ1611.2.K83 1986   158'.1   86-153
ISBN 0-87322-900-2

Developmental Editor: Linda Anne Bump
Copy Editor: Olga Murphy
Production Director: Ernie Noa
Typesetter: Brad Colson
Text Design: Julie Szamocki
Text Layout: Janet Davenport
Cover Photography: © 1986 Dave Black
Cover Design: Jack W. Davis
Printed by: United Graphics

ISBN: 0-87322-900-2
Copyright © 1986 by Tom Kubistant

Printed in the United States of America

10 9 8 7 6 5 4 3 2 1

Published by Life Enhancement Publications
A Division of Human Kinetics Publishers, Inc.
Box 5076, Champaign, IL 61820

Contents

Preface

I was the one who always choked. When the going got tough, I folded. Like many of you, I can vividly recall horror stories of being so nervous during a recital that I could not blow my trumpet or, when on the verge of winning a competition, becoming so frightened that I would lose my concentration and actually find new ways to let victory escape. There was little joy in performing when I always had to battle my inner "demons."

In spite of all of this, I was persistent. Even though I still choked, I became more proficient at my activites. Being the omnipresent analyzer, I was always observing, formulating, and experimenting. As I improved, I gained access to many elite performers and took advantage of this opportunity by interviewing them about their concentration while performing. To my surprise most were eager to discuss their performances. Seemingly, few of them ever had such a chance to verbalize about how they performed, particularly under pressure.

Then one day an athlete asked *me* to help her perform better. Imagine me, the Grand Choker, helping another choker! I quickly discovered that most athletes, performers, coaches, and teachers know now very little about the actual processes of performing. Sure, they know about learning, skill development, training techniques, practice schedules, leadership, motivation, morale, and group dynamics; but when it comes to retaining these skills and producing them in an integrated, consistent, and effective manner, most of them usually cross their fingers and hope for the best.

Thus, I began working with a wide variety of athletes. We explored how they concentrated and performed, especially in stressful situations. Soon, I branched out and began to analyze *how* performing artists achieved such consistently high results. Starting with a variety of musicians, artists, dancers, actors, speakers, and even pageant contestants and tournament poker players, I further expanded my work to include business executives, managers, supervisors, and salespeople. Throughout all of this, I discovered that most of these diverse performers possessed similarities in the ways they produced their skills and knowledge. Although unique styles and activity-specific emphases (such as amplitude for gymnasts, line for dancers and figure skaters, and enunciation for speakers) were apparent, it was also clear that these performers shared many commonalities in their essential beliefs, and approaches to concentrating and performing.

An important discovery I made from working with these high-achievers was that all of us, no matter the ability, have a unique and personal formula for performing well. Each of us must do essential things—both physical and mental—in order to give our best efforts. The problem is that most of us are unaware of all the components of our formulas.

Discovering the components of our individual best performances is the focus of this book. The basic commonalities, principles, and components of performing well are explored so that you can become more aware of and be able to utilize your personal performance formulas. This book is not merely intended for world-class athletes but rather is written to reach people from all walks of life so that they can learn these components and effectively apply them to their own pursuits. Whether it is playing the piano, taking a test, giving a sales presentation, or playing golf, you can learn many things that will heighten the levels and improve the consistency of your performances.

Many of these principles and examples of high-level performing may trigger some reflecting or "aha" responses. This is good because it shows that you can more easily integrate this knowledge into your performing style. However, some of these principles may not be new or surprising at all, and that is even better. All of us need to occasionally remind ourselves of the things we must do to perform well. Because there is very little of the magical, mystical, or esoteric in concentrating and performing well, we can have more control and influence over our performance than we think.

Niels Bohr, a great physicist in the early part of this century, used to begin each semester by saying to his classes, "Whatever I say in here is meant to be a challenge to you. Do not accept anything I say on face value. Rather, think about what I say, ask questions, and then accept what fits for you. But do not dismiss that which does not fit. Store that knowledge away." To you, I issue the same challenge: Do not mindlessly accept or reject anything I say, but be critical about what I present and continually strive to apply this information. The best way to become more aware of your unique performance formula is to carefully weigh everything I say to see how it fits with your beliefs, values, and experiences.

A common attribute among many high-level achievers is that they do not trust their memories. They are always writing down thoughts, ideas, or possible solutions to problems. Many of us may also have had brilliant insights about something—when words or ideas come together in a perfect way—only to later forget them because we didn't write them down. As you read this, write down all the important thoughts, ideas, and applications that come to your mind about performing better. You may even want to maintain a special journal for your thoughts. The physical act of writing something down aids in retention as well as adds commitment to that idea. My intent is for you to actively participate in your learning about performing.

This book is divided into two general parts. In the first half the more theoretical issues of concentration and performance are explored. In the second half practical approaches, techniques, and strategies that you can apply to your performances are presented. At the end of each chapter is a summary of the performance skills covered as well as space to make notes so that you can further define your performance formula and list practical applications.

Many wonderful people have been involved in the development of this book and I would like to thank each of them for their efforts: first and foremost, to Clare Parre for her editing, typing, love, and for showing me how to use the dictionary; to Pearl and David Phoenix, Anna Veltri, Ron Broderdorf, Debby Craun, and Pat Miltenberger for their continual inspiration, support, and sanctuary; to Tom Vasile for his penetrating mind and for his mercy in not hitting me too often on the racquetball court; to Rainer Martens, Linda Bump, and the staff at Human Kinetics Publishers for their ongoing support, encouragement, patience, and commitment to this project; and most of all, to all those marvelous athletes, performing artists, and business people with whom I have worked. Their courage, dedication, creativity, and openness have shown the way for the rest of us.

chapter 1

Overture

The biggest room in the world is the room for improvement.
—Angelo Siciliano (Charles Atlas)

We perform every day. Whether it be an athletic event or cooking, a recital or singing in the shower, taking an examination or making a presentation at a business meeting, we perform. Most of us think that performing is something artificial and formal. On the contrary, performing is just as natural and necessary to us as is learning. Although there is some valid overlap, the processes of learning and remembering are quite separate from the process of performing. Just because I have learned something does not ensure that I will be able to produce the desired product, especially in an integrated and consistent manner.

Throughout our formal education and life experiences, most of us can say that we have learned many skills, competencies, and wisdoms. Beyond that, some of us might have retained and remembered a few of these learnings. Beyond even that, we indeed can consider ourselves fortunate if we have learned how to learn. But very few of us have ever learned how to produce, how to exhibit our skills, or how to perform.

Most of our teachers and coaches believed that performing was just the opposite process of learning. Performance was the "regurgitation of knowledge" syndrome coming into practice. It was assumed that if something was learned, it could be remembered; if it was "in there," it could come out just in the reverse way that it went in. Anyone who has ever choked on an examination or has frozen during a presentation can attest to the fact that just because one knows the material does not ensure that it can be demonstrated in an effective and coherent manner.

Learning and performing are separate but complementary processes. If each process is done well, we can not only become more proficient in that particular process, but we can strengthen the effectiveness of the other process as well. That is, if I know how to learn well, I can be in a better position to perform what I have learned, and if I can perform well, I can be in a better position to learn new things.

Your Personal Performance Formula

Each of us has a unique formula for performing well. However, if asked what that formula is, most of us would usually respond with shrugged shoulders. In surveying numerous divergent performers at all skill levels about what they felt they needed in order to perform well, most responded with such vague generalities as *confidence, preparation, execution,* and *psyching up.* When questioned about the meaning of these words, few could respond.

The major reason why few of us are aware of our personal performance formulas is that we only think about them when we do not perform well. Most of us are aware of the major factors such as incomplete preparation, poor attitudes, lack of attention to details, minimal experience, and low-skill levels that impede our efforts. Some of us may even be aware of some of the more subtle impediments to our performances: for example, pressures to win, self-doubts, fears, the misappropriation of energy, unspecified or unrealistic goals, and the lack of trust in self. An awareness of these impediments as well as their correction are essential components to any of our formulas for performing well. However, there is much more to our performance formulas than minimizing mistakes and errors—but exactly what?

Thinking about what impedes our performances is useful, but let's take this one step further and phrase these efforts in terms of what we need to do instead of what we need to avoid. Any formula in chemistry or physics is composed of the essential components, not the things that are not needed. For example, Einstein's $E=mc^2$ (energy equals mass at the speed of light squared) was written simply and directly. It was not written Energy = the absence of heat, gravity, and wind plus a little mc^2 thrown in for good measure!

In developing your own formula for high-level performing, use the same constructive approach that the hard sciences employ. In the space below (or in your performance journal), use positive words to write down the major components, elements, qualities, attributes, and emphases in your personal performance formula. Go ahead and do it!

Consistently High-Level Performances = _____ +

_____ + _____ +

_____ + _____ +

_____ + _____ +

_____ + _____ .

For many of you, this exercise might have been more difficult than anticipated. That's okay. If you felt that something was missing but could not find the right words for it, return to this page after you have read this chapter and after you have completed this book to see if you can add to your formula.

Formulas are meant to be used. As they are used, they are also meant to be modified and expanded. Feel free to continually change and add to your personal performance formula. I know a runner who now has 19 factors in his formula, a dancer who has 23, and a saleswoman who has 30! These people rely on their formulas to remind themselves of the things they need to emphasize to do well, and so should you.

Needs

We all have the need to do well. Given the opportunity, all of us would want to do our best. We want to take pride in a job well done. However, pressures and stresses, organizational and competitive structures, and self-limiting beliefs frequently divert us away from this need to do a good job.

Whether it is selling an insurance policy, playing volleyball, or giving a recital, performing is an opportunity to prove to ourselves and others that we have developed new knowledge and skills. You see, it is one thing to know something; it is quite another thing to prove this knowledge by applying and producing it. Performing is a concrete proving ground to exhibit our knowledge, skills, and abilities. In doing so, we also have an opportunity to better understand our personal needs.

Abraham Maslow, one of the pioneers of modern psychology, is probably most remembered for his theory outlining the basic needs of the human being (1968). He arranged his schema of needs into a hierarchy in which lower order needs had to be satisfied before one could strive to meet the higher order needs. Maslow's hierarchy ascended from a base of life/physiological needs (such as food, water, heat, clothes, and shelter), to the needs for safety and security, belongingness and affection, respect from others and self-respect, and culminated with his famous concept of "self-actualization." He viewed self-actualization as that need to maximize all of our capabilities.

Another pioneering psychologist, Andras Angyal (1965), consolidated all human needs into two categories: mastery and participation. Angyal believed that we all need to develop competencies and to be in control, but that we also need to feel a part of a group and contribute to the whole. He felt these two basic needs complemented each other and said, "Our needs for mastery are embedded in our longings for participation" (p. 29). According to Angyal, a common ground for meeting both of these basic needs is through extending self and achieving goals.

Both of these views of basic needs imply that the best way to meet needs is to go through a continual cycle of learning, integrating, and producing. As we become more aware of our needs, we learn more about the reasons and meanings attached to them. And as we have more of the reasons and meanings, we see how important performing is to our overall development as individuals. Through performance we not only achieve greater understanding of our needs and how to meet them, but also tap into more of our potentials—the possibilities of what we can become. Performing in everyday structured and unstructured situations is an integral part of the process of self-actualization.

Potential

One of the most misleading and abused concepts in any kind of performance is the word *potential*. Coaches, teachers, and managers often say, "She is not reaching up to her potential," "He has so much potential," and "She has the potential to be an effective supervisor." It is as if they were referring to some kind of measurable entity. Potential is not real. It is simply that: potential.

Most studies on this subject conclude by stating that in a lifetime, a person can only actualize somewhere between 5% and 20% of his or her potential. What happens to the other 80% to 95%? Because potential is unknown, we really do not know how much we have, but we will never know what we have until we seek to actualize it. Morehouse and Gross (1977) expressed the notion of potential in this way:

> The better performer lies dormant in us for three basic reasons. The first is that the various cultural and social forces have conspired to keep it hidden. The second is that it doesn't believe in itself. The third is that it literally doesn't know how to make use of potential. (p.11)

The danger with this conception of potential is that focusing on it alone really becomes self-limiting and, in the long run, self-defeating. Remember some of those high school classmates who seemed to have such great abilities, talents, and potentials, but never amounted to much? On the other hand, there were many who initially did not seem to have the obvious potentials, but through some combination of courage, creativity, dedication, and persistence, achieved much more than those who just sat around on their potentials.

High-level performers from all pursuits do not give much attention to their potentials; instead, they focus on what they can do or achieve here and now. They do not have control over how much potential they have; however, they *do* have control over what they can bring into actuality.

We have a need to become all that we can be. This is the essence of Maslow's need for self-actualization. In this sense, performing, producing, exhibiting, and proving take on much more expanded and important functions than rote regurgitation of disjointed skills or techniques. As there are frustrations and disappointments in not being able to produce, so there are joys and satisfactions in being able to perform consistently well. Morehouse and Gross (1977) further stated that "We resemble our performance and our performance resembles us" (p. 53). No matter what our roles and functions are in life, how we perform is as crucial to our successes and development as individuals as the outcomes of our performances. These efforts define who we are as well as give us indications of what we can become.

The Quest

Our quests to improve ourselves are just as valid for the weekend warrior as for the professional athlete, the business person as well as the homemaker, and the student as well as the teacher. Performing is a proving ground that provides us with information about what we can do well and about what we need to do to improve.

The Soviets call their science of sports and performance psychology *anthropomaximology,* which means "the study of human maximums." World-wide, people are studying how human beings perform, especially under pressure. From this research, a body of knowledge that is establishing basic principles of high-level performance has evolved. These principles are being derived from the commonalities exhibited by athletes, artists, business people, astronauts, and kids on the playgrounds.

A systematic program to develop the necessary skills for improving your performances is presented in this book. Whether you want to concentrate better, to maximize more of your potential, to give more consistent performances, to improve personal productivity, or to feel more satisfied with your efforts, the applicable approaches presented here will help you accomplish your goals. The more emphasis placed on developing skills, the better the performance. The great baseball pitcher Satchel Paige was renowned for saying, "Don't look over your shoulder . . . someone may be gaining on you!" When we look ahead, we run better than if we were looking back, which is the theme of this book. If we look ahead to improving our efforts, we will perform much better than if we were always backstepping to solve our problems.

Development is the best problem solver. If we continually spend all our time trying to solve problems, we frequently lose perspective of what we need to do in order to excel. Business people call this inefficient process "management by putting out brushfires." That is, many of us spend so much time rushing about to solve problems that we lose sight of where we need to go. By emphasizing what things we need to do well, problems are often averted, take care of themselves, or are minimized. With this developmental perspective, you will be in a much better position to understand and overcome performance problems when you experience them.

If you discover a particular performance problem while reading this book, start by asking yourself what things you are not doing well that generated this problem. Next, ask yourself what specific approaches and techniques must be emphasized to get back on course—then do it.

The biggest room in the world is, indeed, the room for improvement, and this book is a laboratory for that room.

Chapter 1 Performance Skills

- Learning and performing are separate and complementary processes. Performing is as crucial as learning to the development of the self-actualized person.

- Each of us has a personal performance formula. Become more aware of yours and continually update it.

- What needs do you meet by performing, competing, or producing?

- What things are you doing today that you could only dream about 10 years ago?

  _____

  _____

  _____

  Don't worry about your potentials. Rather, emphasize that which you have control over and can do now.

- Development is the best problem solver. Continually look ahead and focus on improvement through developing skills. By doing so, you will minimize performance problems. Furthermore, those performance problems you do encounter will be more readily resolved, allowing you to return to the things you need to do.

- Notes: _____

  _____

  _____

  _____

  _____

- Additions or changes to your personal performance formula:

  _____

  _____

  _____

  _____

chapter 2

The Zones of Performance

Gee Toto, I don't think we're in Kansas anymore.
—Dorothy in Wizard of Oz

Any exploration into how to perform better must begin with a review of the types, or levels, of performing. Most of us have not thought much about the various types of performances. We say we go out there to do our best or to win, but beyond that, there is little knowledge about performing.

Assessment of Different Performances

Think about your particular sport, business, or performance specialty and see how many different types, kinds, or levels of performance you can identify. Write them down here:

_____   _____   _____

_____   _____   _____

_____   _____   _____

_____   _____   _____

Were the types of performances you thought about first and for which you have the most labels your disappointing efforts? You might have come up with "poor performances," "lackluster performances," "inconsistent performances," "flat performances," "choked performances," "mediocre performances," "disastrous performances," or just plain "failures." Some of you might have identified different dimensions of performance such as "individual performance," "team performance," "lucky performance," or even "fluke performance." Were your smallest number of types, or levels, of performance for positive efforts? You might have come up with "win," "success," or "outstanding performance," but beyond that, you were probably unable to be more specific.

The reason why many types, or levels, of positive efforts are included is because most of us do not really know what we want to achieve in our performances. Beyond nice, general goals like winning or success, most of us approach our performances, simply hoping for the best or praying we don't make fools out of ourselves. Dancers have a good system of viewing their performances: That is, for any given program, they see three different performances—the one planned, the one given, and the one they wish they had given. Sometimes, searching for a good performance is like searching for the Golden Fleece: It is in view, but it is always just out of reach.

Having a better understanding of the types, or levels, of good performances, we are better able to plan more specific goals for effective performance. Good performances fall into three general categories or zones: optimal, maximal, and peak performances. These zones overlap a little, but there are basic distinctions between them. The performance zones are like the gears in an automobile transmission: Each one has its own range and function, but they must all be used to efficiently reach a destination. Understanding these three zones of performance is critical for improved and for more consistent performing. Let's explore each of these more thoroughly.

Optimal and Maximal Performances

Optimal and maximal performances are the two major forms of high-level performance. Together, they comprise about 95% of positive efforts. Although the overlap that exists between these two zones results in some understandable confusion, optimal and maximal performances have many separate characteristics.

Webster's New Collegiate Dictionary defines *optimum* as "the amount or degree of something that is most favorable to some end." It defines *maximum* as "the greatest quantity or value attained," and "the period of highest, greatest, or utmost development." Both of these performance dimensions seek the best. However, my definitions differ. I define optimal performing as *that which attains the most consistent and efficient results;* and I define maximal performing as *that which attains the greatest results one's abilities and experiences can provide, regardless of the costs.*

For example, those of you who do any kind of aerobic exercising know that there is an optimal heart rate zone in which you can achieve the best cardiovascular conditioning. When I am in this zone, I am achieving my most effective cardiovascular conditioning with little wear and tear on my body. My optimal heart rate zone is between 148 and 160 beats per minute (bpm). During a training session, if my heart rate is, for example, only 110 bpm, I am not achieving all the exercise benefits I had planned. Conversely, if my heart rate is 190 bpm, I have definitely overextended myself, and the exercise is becoming counterproductive to my cardiovascular and recuperative systems.

An automobile is another good example to use in explaining these zones. Today's automobiles are designed and engineered so that most of their optimal zones of functioning are between 45 to 55 mph. In this zone the car is achieving its best gas mileage with minimal wear and tear. Sure, I can "push the pedal to the metal" and go 90 mph. This is a maximal zone of performance. At this speed I can arrive at my destination sooner, but this zone has produced such negative effects as poorer gas mileage, overheating, the oil breaking down faster, and greater overall wear and tear on all the systems.

A big game, an important recital, a try-out, or a job interview are some situations in which a maximal performance is desired, regardless of the mental and physical costs. To a large degree, the ability to produce a maximal performance is dependent on previous optimal performances. Optimal performances build up the specific skills and endurance levels in our specialty so that we are better able to give maximal performances. It would be foolish for me to try and run a 3-hour marathon (maximal performance) without putting in a series of quality training runs (optimal performances).

Maximal performances achieve goals and extend personal frontiers, but due to the demanding nature of these efforts, they have depleting mental and physical effects on the performer. It is for this reason that maximal performances should be planned and spaced, with ample time given to recover from them. For example, elite American swimmers have to plan to give maximal performances for their college championships, national championships, world championships, the Pan American Games, the Olympic trials, and the actual Olympic Games. Especially during Olympic years these athletes have to plan their maximal efforts to allow enough time to recuperate and prepare for the next effort. Without such planning and pacing, the chances are that they will overtrain and give flat performances.

Optimal and maximal performances can also be distinguished by the factor of experience. Experience in the same or in similar situations is an essential component to any high-level performance. If I have never been in a particular performing situation, it would be foolish to expect a maximal (i.e., a 100% effective) performance because I probably wouldn't even know what a maximal performance meant. Putting pressure on myself to give a maximal effort will simply serve to sabotage my efforts. Even if I did have limited experiences in a particular performing situation, a more realistic performance goal might be 70%, or even 50% of my maximum effort. That 70% could be considered optimal in this given performance. I am producing to the best of my abilities, and I am also learning skills and approaches I can use later. As I gained additional experience, it would then be realistic to set these percentages progressively higher. Gaining experience through a series of optimal efforts is precisely the rationale behind role playing, practice tests, mock trials, and dress rehearsals. Optimal performances, then, act like springboards to increase the momentum toward future optimal and, eventually, maximal performances.

One of the most pervasive and most destructive fallacies in sport or business is the expectation that one must produce

100% (maximal) performances all the time. Some coaches and managers even extend this absurdity to demanding 101%, 110%, or 150% efforts. This myopic view of performance simply serves to advance the additional fallacies that (a) the only adjustment that can be made is to always try harder, and (b) more is always better. These destructive views of performance can only lead to frustration, stagnation, self-imposed limitations, and eventually, poorer performances, injuries, and self-defeat. Especially at higher levels of competencies, more is rarely better.

An increasing number of business and political leaders are utilizing the notions of optimal and maximal efforts in the supervision of their subordinates. Many of these supervisors used to push their people harder and harder by giving them more and more to do. While this might have worked in the short run, the workers eventually became overly stressed, demoralized, and burned out so that no amount of incentives or urging could inspire them. Wise leaders now realize that overall high levels of individual performance and organizational productivity are composed of optimal and of maximal efforts, as well as recuperation and easy times.

Optimal performances need not always be seen as stepping stones to maximal performances. Quite often, optimal performances are goals in themselves. During these efforts, one can focus, practice, and refine one or two components. I do not want to give the impression that optimal performances are often as intense as maximal performances, but their goals are more means oriented while maximal performances are usually ends in themselves. Optimal performances are designed as consistent, progressive, integrative, efficient, and effective efforts that can be ends in themselves and/or be means to other ends.

Maximal performances, on the other hand, are designed to achieve the greatest or best quantity, value, or degree of results, regardless of the expenditures. Maximal performances extend frontiers of accomplishment and establish new goals for future efforts. In this sense, maximal performances can be seen as a complementary spiral that improves the overall level of consistency of effort. As these two zones continue to ascend, they pave the way to the stratosphere of high-level performing—the peak performance.

Peak Performance

Think back to the incredible performances you have witnessed in your lifetime. In sports, remember when Roger Bannister broke the 4-minute mile? When Joe DiMaggio had a 56-game hitting streak? When Bob Beamon jumped 29 ft, 2-1/2 in. at the 1968 Olympics? When the 1969 Mets won the World Series? When Mark Spitz broke seven world records on his way to winning seven gold medals at the 1972 Olympics? How about Franz Klammer's unbelievable downhill run at the 1976 Winter Olympics, or Eric Heiden's five gold medals in speed skating at Lake Placid in 1980? The United States' Olympic hockey teams of 1960 and 1980? Jane Torvill and Christopher Dean's perfection in ice dancing at the 1984 Winter Olympics? Or your son going 5 for 5 last Saturday? In other realms, do you remember Martin Luther King's "I Have A Dream" speech? Lee Iacocca's transformation of Chrysler Corporation? Mikhail Baryshnikov's complete mastery in "Swan Lake?" Jesse Jackson's "I am . . . Somebody" speech? Or Sir Laurence Olivier in any Shakespearian play? All are excellent examples of peak performances.

Now think back to your own great, unforgettable performances. Remember those times when everything came together, seemed to click, and in which you had complete control? Those times could have been when you felt you could hit the golf ball exactly anywhere you wanted or when you had complete control of an audience or when a tennis ball seemed to be as big as a beach ball and it was hard not to hit lines. Those times could have also been when your dance steps magically came together to produce new levels of artistry or when you were in such command of your sales presentation that you had the prospects eating out of your hand or when you instinctively knew how to play each poker hand. These memorable occasions prompt us to wonder just how far we can go and provide us with the incentives to find out. They are called peak performances and are the times when you transcend all previous efforts, when you seem to have both no control and yet super control over what is happening, and when you don't understand anything yet comprehend everything. In short, these are the performances you have always dreamed about.

The term peak performance is a derivative of Maslow's (1968) "peak experience." Maslow saw such experiences as those rare times in which we transcend into states of beauty, awe, wonder, bliss, clarity, simplicity, calm, order, understanding, and wisdom, to name a few. Frequently unplanned and unpredictable, these experiences are quantum leaps of integration and synthesis, extending you and your performances into new frontiers.

With respect to performance, peak performances are times in which the results are much more than the sum of the individual skills, abilities, and experiences. Peak performances can range from a 10-second sprint all the way to a month-long winning streak. Murphy and White (1978) summarized the range of these peak experiences in sports as follows:

> In hundreds of reports from athletes, we have found that the sport experience produces many unusual feelings and ideas. We have noted sixty or more kinds of sensations in the sports, from a simple sense of well-being to exotic movements when the body seems to stop time, or change shape, or free the self to travel out of the body. (p. 10)

They went on to describe some of these sensations:

> Their accounts support each other: men and women in very different sports tell stories that are quite similar. Their experiences range from surges of speed and power to movements of mystery and awe, from ecstasy to peace and calm, from intrinsic right action to intimations of immorality, from detachment and perfect freedom to a sense of unity with all things, from a comfortable feeling of being "at home" to uncanny incidents when the body, as if weightless, tells the brain that it has taken up floating or flying. (p. 11)

Strange? Eerie? Yes. Most performers of all ability levels have experienced varying degrees of these sensations. Many runners, dancers, and skiers have experienced a "high" in which they seem to float. Many football, hockey, and soccer players have experienced times of great unity with their teammates in which the synchronization of movements and innate communication were uncannily precise. In the midst of the chaos of backstage, many actors and musicians have experienced sensations of peace and calm in which they intuitively knew that their performance would be better than ever before. Many professional speakers and sales-people have experienced occasions when their presentations seemed to flow in such a way that the speaker and receiver were on exactly the same mental wavelength and the message was anticipated even before it was said. Whatever forms they take, peak performances are more common than most of us realize.

Sometimes it is difficult to distinguish peak performances from dominance. Occasionally, an outstanding athlete or performing artist will emerge who so outshines his or her colleagues that he or she redefines new standards in excellence. These new standards set by elite performers often cause confusion among other performers in regard to what peak performances are to them, but such is the nature of dominance. Greg Louganis in springboard and platform diving, Edwin Moses in the 400-meter hurdles, Luciano Pavarotti in operas, and Martina Navratilova in tennis are examples of such dominance. They are simply operating on different levels than their colleagues.

One of the hallmarks of the peak performance is an alteration of perceptions. Our "normal" ways of perceiving and functioning seem to shift perspectives. The following are the major categories of these alterations:

1. Time seems to shift into slow motion, yet the event seems to go by so quickly. Golfers, bowlers, and baseball pitchers and batters have all reported that during such times, they seem to have all the time in the world to make minute adjustments and attend to all the details of their actions. Endurance radically improves. Marathon runners and triathletes have reported how they seem to have vast storehouses of energy, feeling as if they could go on for days. Writers, composers, and artists have noted how they achieved extreme levels of concentration for hours when they were creating something outstanding.

2. Shapes and colors change. Martial arts students and football defensive backs have reported how their opponents seemed to change shape to allude them. Observers of figure skating have noted how sometimes a performer was just a blur and seemed to cover unbelievable distances during jumps and leaps. Those experiencing peak performances also reported how familiar colors seem to strangely alter or change altogether. These

alterations almost always coincide with shifts in time perspectives.

3. Sizes and weights change. Weight and power lifters and shot put, javelin, and discus throwers have reported times when their objects seemed so light that they felt they could lift or throw any weight any distance. Golfers, tennis and racquetball players, and baseball hitters said that there were times when their implements became so light and diffuse that they almost seemed to become a natural extension of their arms, so much so that they could not distinguish where their hands left off and the implements began.

4. The senses become super alert and acute. Batters and tennis players have reported how they could see the seams of the ball, orchestra conductors have experienced times when they could hear every note from every instrument, football defensive players have stated that there were times when they could hear the play being called in the opponents' huddle 15 yards away, and many various athletes and business people have reported that they could actually taste victory or smell fear in their opponents!

Why then, don't we hear more about these peak performances and experiences? There are many reasons. First, these experiences occur so relatively infrequently that it is very difficult to generalize them. Second, they are so unique that very often there just aren't enough words to accurately describe them. Third, and probably most common, the performer does not know what to make of them and will rarely talk about them for fear of being thought of as crazy.

Despite what coaches, teachers, and writers say, peak performances cannot be summoned at will, nor can they be predicted. A myriad of factors must be combined in the right proportions, at the right times, and in the right settings to produce a peak performance. Although they vary with the individual and the activity, the following factors are necessary in producing a peak performance: previous optimal training experiences, proper mental preparation, pacing, prioritizing energy, unquestioning belief in self, accurate planning and goal setting, seeing and taking advantage of opportunities, honoring and maximizing one's own unique skills, luck, successful past performances, proper nutrition, making sense of prior peak performances, proper rest and recuperation, patience, persistence, maintaining a sense of joy and fun, and balance in lifestyle. Many factors that must be present in the proper combinations are still missing from our recipe for a peak performance to occur. These missing factors are the quests of performance psychologists, coaches, business people, and performers alike.

Within recent years, more of these pieces of the puzzle of peak performance have been falling into place. Although peak performances still cannot be predicted, plans can be made so that there is a better chance of them occurring. Undoubtedly, one of the most important factors necessary to attain a peak performance is a good understanding of one's own personal performance formula. The more you are aware of the things you need to do well, the better the chances you will have to synthesize them into a peak performance. This is why the personal performance formula has been emphasized so much.

However and whenever they occur, peak performances, breaking barriers and limitations, set the standards for future efforts. As training techniques and programs become more sophisticated and refined, the integration with such other disciplines as transpersonal psychology, nutrition, leadership, and exercise physiology becomes more complete. As the achievements of courageous individual performers become more frequently reported, peak performances will become less abstract and mysterious and more planned and predictable.

Conclusion

Optimal, maximal, and peak zones of performance are the metaphorical gears we employ to drive ourselves to excel. These zones provide us with the parameters of functioning from which we can develop and apply the psychological skills necessary to perform and produce at our best. As we understand more about these different types of performance zones and how to use them, we will be better able to improve both the levels and consistencies of our performances.

Chapter 2 Performance Skills

- High-level performing occupies different zones of functioning. How does this breakdown of optimal, maximal, and peak performance fit with your conceptions?

  _____

  _____

  _____

  _____

- Although there is some overlap between the two zones, optimal performance is characterized by efficient functioning most often as a means to something else, whereas maximal performance is characterized by an all-out effort for the best results, no matter the price. What is optimal performing for you? What is maximal performing? What interplay do they have in your notions of high-level performing?

  _____

  _____

  _____

  _____

- What are some of the words, sensations, and feelings that are representative of your peak performance?

  _____

  _____

  _____

  _____

- List some of the elements in your personal performance formula that you have found to be necessary to put you in the best position to give a/an

  Optimal performance _____

  _____

Maximal performance _____

_____

Peak performance _____

_____

- Notes: _____

_____

_____

_____

_____

_____

- Additions or changes to your personal performance formula:

_____

_____

_____

_____

_____

_____

c h a p t e r   3

Attitudes and Artichokes

We become what we think about.
—Earl Nightengale

The single greatest commonality I have found among high-level performers, athletes, and business people is their unshakeable yet realistically positive attitudes about themselves and their existing situations. These people are quite aware of the subtle yet powerful effects their attitudes and beliefs can have on their efforts. At one time or another, most of them have suffered devastating effects of negative attitudes on their performances. From these painful and disappointing experiences, they have found that it is always more beneficial and satisfying to be positive.

I was struck with the depth of this unswerving belief in self when I talked with Phil Mahre in 1982. He had just returned to the United States after successfully defending his All-Around World Cup skiing championship title. Humbly yet assuredly, Phil stated, "In a race someone would have to be in super form on a certain day to beat me. And if he does, more power to him." Phil may not exactly know just how he is going to win, but he always knows he will give his best effort.

Attitudes

"He's got a poor attitude." "Her attitude is holding her back." "The team has an attitude problem." How often have you heard these kinds of phrases and wondered just what they really meant? The term *attitude* has often been a catch-all word for the myriad of mental processes involved in performance. For those coaches, teachers, business people, and journalists who are unwilling or unable to take the time and effort to explore the mental processes of performing, attitude is a convenient dumping ground. After a while, the word *attitude* could be replaced by the word *artichoke* with about just as much meaning!

Attitudes are thoughts, feelings, and intuitions about ourselves that are derived from our views of a situation, from our past experiences, and from our goals and aspirations. Our attitudes reflect our basic beliefs in how we approach the world. Krause (1980) expanded upon this notion stating that "*Attitudes* help us determine *perceptions* of the world, which in turn affect our immediate *feelings* which have a lot to do with our *performance*" (p. 47). In short, attitudes are an ever-changing set of constructs about ourselves that both release and direct our performance energies.

Essential Choices

In an era where there are more complexities, options, possibilities, and shades of gray, it is refreshing to discover that our performance attitudes can only take one of two forms: Either we can be positive and build ourselves up, or we can be negative and drag ourselves down. There are no exceptions, no middle ground, and no qualifications.

Top performers from all fields realize they have essential choices to make in every situation they face. These people actively choose to be positive. They do not adopt pie-in-the-sky or wishing-and-hoping mentalities. Rather, given a set of circumstances or a performance situation, they adopt a realistically positive outlook. They know how powerful the combination of a realistic view and optimism can be.

When I hear business people, athletes, or performing artists say, "Sure, I know a positive mental attitude is important, but . . .," I know they really don't believe it as much as they could. This "yes, but" mind set is actually a covert form of pessimism as is the indecisiveness of a person who is not sure of whether he or she has a positive or a negative attitude. Because pessimism is sneaky and subtle, we must continually build ourselves up, expecially in performing situations. If we do not, then we are covertly dragging ourselves down. It is as simple as that.

A realistic and consistent positive mental attitude is dependent on our perspectives. Some of you may remember that back in the 1960s there was a television commercial for the Peace Corps that showed a half glass of water similar to the one shown in Figure 3.1. The announcer asked, "Do

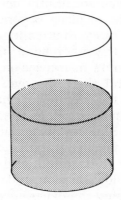

Figure 3.1   Is this glass half full or half empty?

you see this glass as half full or half empty?" He continued to say, "If you see it as half full, the Peace Corps is interested in talking with you." High-level performers always view their personal glasses of water as half full. They focus and build on what they have going for them. This does not mean they are ego-centered or narcissistic; rather, they recognize and reinforce what they have. While the pessimist continually focuses on what he or she is lacking, does not do well, or is deficient in, the optimist realistically focuses on what he or she already possesses and uses it as a solid foundation.

A couple of years ago I worked with two talented young women who were rehearsing a complicated piano duet a week prior to the performance. They seemed to have the same skills and abilities, and were even having problems with the same parts of the composition. The distinguishing characteristic, however, was attitude. One pianist was continually saying, "I'll never get this right," "This is impossible," "I'd like to give up and run away," "I know I will embarrass myself and let down my partner and teacher on Saturday night," and "This failure will prove to everyone that I am a fraud and a worthless pianist." In contrast, the other pianist was always telling herself, "Hey, I understand this section better today than I did yesterday," "At least I muddled through that difficult part better today," and "Any mediocre piano player can play something simple. It is a challenge of how good I am—and can become—to see how well I can master something that is difficult."

You can probably guess what happened on recital night. The pianist who was constantly pessimistic and fearful made major errors in the piece. Beyond that, she lacked the style, rhythm, and range that distinguished good pianists from the rest. On the other hand, the pianist who was actively optimistic and who focused on improvement played better in the recital than she ever did in any of the rehearsals. She told me later that she had made up her mind that she had prepared as well as she could and could not practice any more. She was going out there to do the best possible job and be satisfied with that. She had also decided that she was going to have fun, and it showed, for there seemed to be more flow, passion, and poise—she genuinely seemed to be enjoying the experience.

Most coaches, teachers, and managers probably have experienced similar situations. Given equal abilities, experiences, and preparation, it is usually the performer's positive attitudes about self and the situation that act as catalysts to integrating skills, releasing energies, and determining the quality of the overall performance. David Phoenix, a colleague of mine, has devised the chart shown in Figure 3.2 to relate the degree of positiveness of attitudes to the chances for success.

If you think you can do something, you have a much better chance for success than if you wish you could. Even if you think you might be able to do something, you still have a much better chance for success than if you don't know how.

Developing the Habit of Positiveness

What many of us do not realize is that it takes much more courage, creativity, dedication, and conscious awareness to be positive than to be negative. If you sit back and

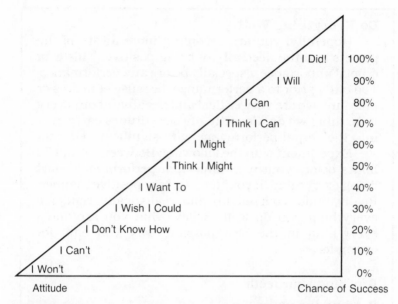

Attitude	Chance of Success
I Did!	100%
I Will	90%
I Can	80%
I Think I Can	70%
I Might	60%
I Think I Might	50%
I Want To	40%
I Wish I Could	30%
I Don't Know How	20%
I Can't	10%
I Won't	0%

Figure 3.2 Degree of positiveness related to chances for success.

do nothing for yourself, you will eventually slip into being ambivalent, apathetic, and pessimistic. Staying positive about yourself and your efforts requires a continual process of consciously affirming and reinforcing yourself.

Many people ask me, "How can I be positive?" My usual response to this is, "By being positive!" There are no preparatory steps—just start looking at the bright side. What this really implies is that you have to make the conscious decision to always view yourself and every situation in the best possible light. With this perspective you can then begin to create a habit of being positive.

First, to establish a realistic and sustaining positive mental attitude, you need to be optimistic, eager, and reinforcing in everyday situations. This attitude establishes the base from which you can become more positive in the more formal and pressurized performance situations. As being positive becomes more ingrained and natural to you, it will become more automatic in all aspects of your life.

Whenever you have doubt or confusion about yourself or a current situation, consciously decide to be optimistic and eager. Pessimism thrives on doubt and confusion. As you acquire the habit of being positive, you will see that responsibility for self, decision making, and optimism all flow together.

Do Everything Well

Hopefully, you are becoming more aware of the powers and the necessity of being positive. This is of crucial importance, especially before any performance. Too often prior to a performance, because of nerves or pressure, we are very critical and negative about every little thing we do. Covertly, these attitudes carry over into the actual performance with significant effects.

Experiment with the following: Between 48 and 72 hours before your next important performance, start doing everything in your life in a very positive manner. Really build yourself up and realistically reinforce everything you do well. Believe that you are doing everything in the best possible way you can, for example:

Brushing your teeth

Reading the paper

Combing your hair

Walking down the stairs

Making an omelet

Listening to a friend

Computing a math problem

Making a left hand turn in your car or on your bicycle.

Writing a letter

Cleaning the house

Performing your event

Positiveness breeds positiveness. After you have been successful with this process, extend this time period to 4 days before your next performance, and then to 1 week.

Performances do not exist in isolation. They are reflective of our essential attitudes, daily practices, and basic views of the rest of the areas of our lives. Being optimistic and positive means being realistically optimistic and positive in all the respects of our lives all the time.

Tearing Down Within a Framework of Building Up

I do not want to give the impression that high-level performers are dreamy Pollyannas. They are, however, realists who continually view themselves in the best light. High-level performers occasionally criticize themselves, but this criticism is placed within the larger context of growth. development, or improvement. There is a difference between tearing down for long-term improvement versus dragging down from pessimism or fear. Tearing down has its place in high-level performance if it is considered in the larger perspective of building up.

Ineffective performers and coaches use criticism as an end in itself; effective performers and coaches use it as a means to improvement. How many times have you seen (or experienced) a football coach, director, or dance teacher, who has constantly berated everyone for weeks, say on the day of the performance, "Okay, now everyone be positive"? How can these performers possibly give a good effort or be positive with this kind of negative input?

Berating usually creates deeper pessimistic attitudes. At the very best, it can only be used to correct a single action. In a larger context, such an approach fosters isolation and segmentation of skills, inhibits integration and continuity of actions, breeds distrust, and promotes fear. In such cases, rather than putting skills together and functioning optimally, the performers' emphases are directed toward not making mistakes. Paradoxically, when we focus on not making particular mistakes, we are actually programming them to occur. For example, if I have been continually criticized for raising my head during a golf swing, I may become so self-conscious of it that I am actually programming myself to raise my head!

Knowledgeable teachers, coaches, leaders, and performers will occasionally tear down, but quite differently than in the previous description. Periodically, we must unlearn a counterproductive or inappropriate action before we can reformulate it. Unlike the process of berating, the productive process of tearing down is a means to a greater end. After I have torn down the counterproductive action, then and only then am I in a position to rechannel the energies of that action into more productive directions. This process of tearing down is, then, a stepping stone toward building up. In the case of raising my head during my golf swing, the more productive process of tearing down would go something like this: I know that raising my head is counterproductive, so in order to make better contact with the ball (positive goals), I must keep my head down all the way through the swing. By keeping my head down, I place myself in a better position for my left shoulder to stay down and my legs to move more fully through the shot (integration with other components). Hence, my swing will be more fluid and powerful (means), and I will achieve better and more consistent results (ends).

When seen as a means to more productive ends—and not as an end in itself—tearing down is a positive process. If we keep our perspectives on learning, growing, and improving, tearing down can be an important aid in our development as performers.

Attitudes in Performance Evaluation

High-level performers have not only learned to employ a perspective of tearing down within a framework of growth and development, but they have also extended these positive attitudes in evaluating their performances. They have expanded their evaluations of their efforts beyond the quantitive result-oriented dimensions of whether or not they won, of their score, or of their ranking. Furthermore, they have discovered that evaluating the means, or processes, to these results was also essential to their overall improvement.

Of course, the results of a performance are important. Performers who say they don't care whether they win or lose are lying to somebody. However, focusing on the results alone is too narrow of an orientation for effective evaluation and long-term improvement.

Quite often performers do not have complete control over the outcomes of their efforts. Team members may make critical mistakes, judges may score questionably, or conditions may be unfavorable. With this in mind, it is important that performers assess those parts of their efforts over which they did have control, regardless of the outcomes. They can assess such factors as success of execution, difficulty of task and response to pressure; they can also assess how well they concentrated and relaxed and what they learned about themselves for use in similar situations.

Any complete evaluation of a performance must take into consideration not only the outcomes, but also the means, or processes, used in achieving those outcomes. A simple way to organize this evaluation is illustrated in the schema presented in Figure 3.3.

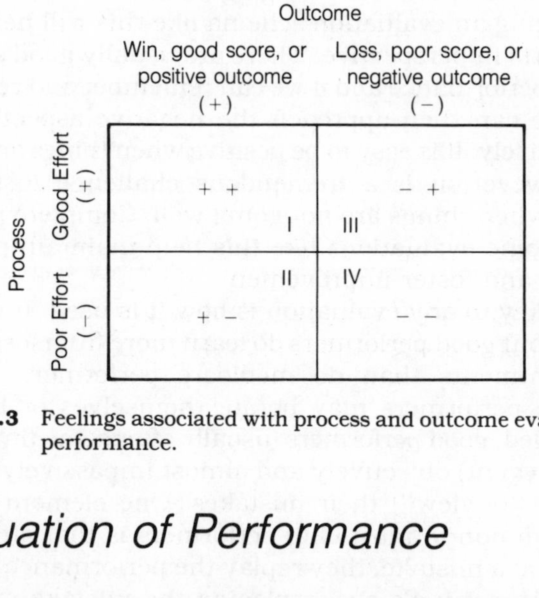

Outcome

		Win, good score, or positive outcome (+)	Loss, poor score, or negative outcome (−)
Process	Good Effort (+)	+ + ⟶ I	− + ⟶ III
	Poor Effort (−)	+ − ⟶ II	− − ⟶ IV

Figure 3.3 Feelings associated with process and outcome evaluation of performance.

Evaluation of Performance

Obviously, the most desirable combination illustrated in Figure 3.3 is in Quadrant I where you performed well and achieved good results. These are the times to pat yourself on the back. It is said that a mark of good performers is that they can achieve good results even when they don't necessarily perform well. This combination is found in Quadrant II. These are the times to thank your lucky stars but to review how you could have performed better. High-level performers have learned to value Quadrant III where they performed well even though the results were disappointing. They often say in such situations, "Hey, I gave it my best shot." Quadrant IV contains the only undesirable combination: The performer's efforts were disappointing and so were the results. These are the times to go back to the drawing board.

For example, after a day of flyfishing, I could evaluate my efforts according to this matrix. If I threw a nice, tight loop where the fly landed softly in the water, and the fish were so impressed that they leaped on my hook—this would fall into Quadrant I. If I casted poorly, but the fish were yawning at the right times—this would fall into Quadrant II. If I casted wonderfully, but the fish did not have enough class to go for my flies—this would fall into Quadrant III. The only bad Quadrant would be IV where I always tangled the line in the trees and the fish giggled at me!

Utilizing an evaluation schema like this will help keep your efforts in perspective. There are usually good aspects in every performance and if we can remember and reinforce them, we can then approach the negative aspects more constructively. It is easy to be positive when things are going well; however, it is a tremendous challenge to remain positive when things are not going well. Complete process and outcome evaluations like this help maintain positive attitudes and foster improvement.

The key to any evaluation is how it is used. It may be a cliche', but good performers do learn more from losses and disappointments than do mediocre performers. Where mediocre performers may berate themselves or become discouraged, good performers (usually after some time away from the event) objectively and almost impassively review (literally, "re-view") their mistakes. One element I have found common to most elite performers is that after they have found a mistake, they replay the performance repeatedly in their mind's eye, replacing the mistake with the correct action. By doing so, they will then be in a better position to perform the proper action whenever a similar situation occurs.

From our school experiences, early training situations, and poor work environments, many of us have learned to be wary and even to avoid evaluations. It has taken many of us awhile to discover that broad, balanced, and nonjudgmental evaluations are tools for better subsequent performances. Viewing evaluations as a means to improvement promotes more constructive uses of it, and as in all components of high-level performance, positiveness breeds positiveness.

Belief and Trust

Our attitudes not only reflect our essential thoughts and feelings about ourselves and our worlds, but also reflect our essential choices of how we approach our performances. Our attitudes are the most outward representations of the deeper and more abstract qualities of belief and trust.

The relief pitcher Tug McGraw is famous for saying, "You gotta believe." Believing in self is the core of any positive attitude. Believing in yourself is a continual process of consciously reaffirming your abilities and qualities. It is also reminding yourself that you like yourself and what you are doing. It is really a very simple proposition: Either you believe in yourself or you don't; and if you don't know, you don't.

I am always amused how beginners and intermediates in just about any activity refuse to trust themselves. They spend all that time and energy learning many skills and then, at the time of the performance, wholeheartedly believe that they know nothing! The resulting performances usually resemble the disconnected movements of mechanical toy soldiers.

One of the great wisdoms that Tim Gallwey taught us in his Inner Game series of books (see Additional Resources listing) is that through proper learning the body knows what to do. What we are really doing in any physical activity during our practicing is giving the opportunity for our muscles to learn the specific movements. this is called muscle memory. The challenge is to trust that the body knows how to move and then to let it perform. Too often we don't know how to trust, so our minds spend a great deal of time and energy checking up on and trying to direct what the body is doing. These efforts only serve to sabotage the performance.

Here is an example of how counterproductive directing and checking up can be. Imagine that I have just learned all the parts of a tennis backhand. Instead of letting the body do what it has learned and giving it a chance to perform the whole action, I would probably be tempted to direct the movements using such subverbal commands as this:

Pivot on the ball of the left foot and at the same time change to the proper backhand grip. Next, cradle the racquet loosely in the off hand and bring it back so that the head of the racquet is pointing directly behind. The shoulders and hips should be in a line extending to where I want to hit the ball. Now, keeping the elbow close to the body, start a level swing, shifting the weight onto the front foot. Keep the racquet face even or slightly above the wrist throughout the stroke. Now lock the elbow, making contact with the ball about 12 inches ahead of the lead foot. Finish with a high follow-through so that the butt of the racquet is pointing down to the ground. And remember, stay relaxed and fluid!

If I thought of all these things, the ball would be past me, collecting cobwebs by the fence!

This kind of directing inhibits the integration of the various skills, impedes a natural outflowing of them, and creates debilitating tension. Most of all, this kind of distrust prevents me from learning how to be relaxed and fluid in my actions. So I could have all the skills and abilities in the world, but by not trusting myself, my actions and performances will be disjointed and inconsistent. It would be like a car hitting only on three cylinders. The bowling great Billy Welu capsulized this entire notion simply by saying, "Trust is a must or your game is a bust."

Many novices say, "If I only trusted myself more, then I could do it," and proceed to wait until they somehow magically obtain the trust. What they don't realize is that trust and belief in self evolve from action. Just let go of the checking up and directing and start doing. Trust and belief will come as results of your actions.

Trust is one of the most overlooked qualities of effective business management. Most novice supervisors have trouble with delegating responsibility because they feel they have to oversee and monitor every step of their workers' progress. The inefficiency of this managerial style is that two or three people are doing work meant for one person. The reason these problems occur is that novice supervisors really don't trust their people, nor, if examined further, do they trust themselves.

On the other hand, effective leaders give their people freedom with assignments by directly and indirectly stating to their subordinates, "I trust you to complete this task," and then allowing them to do it. They do not worry if the workers might not be able to handle it, but will deal with that problem if and when it arises. Good supervisors know that when workers feel trusted, they will perform tasks much more efficiently than if they feel someone is always checking up on them. These leaders are aware that the power of trust can greatly affect worker performance, dedication, loyalty, pride, and even innovation.

For one who does not have trust in self, the concept of letting go may be quite foreign, even scary. Those who try really hard to let go usually fall into the trap of saying, "Okay, now trust," as if they were giving commands to some dog! This only serves to promote the same kinds of mind directing they were trying to undo. I often visualize the processes of checking up and directing as hands that have a chokehold on the skill and knowledge pathways of myself. Letting go means easing off on this chokehold so that I can allow my skills and knowledges to flow out.

In his landmark book, *Zen in the Art of Archery,* Herrigel (1953) hears this from his teacher: "The right shot at the right moment does not come because you do not let go of yourself. You do not wait for fulfillment, but brace yourself for failure" (p. 33). Too often we have our minds trying to focus on too many things at once: all the segments of the action, fears, distractions, expectations, the opposition, possible negative consequences, or even on what we are going to have for dinner. When we do this, checking up and directing is inevitable, and disappointment is assured.

Letting go is allowing your skills, wisdoms, and experiences to emerge from your reservoirs of potential and knowledge in an integrated and fluid manner. Go ahead and let go. After all, how do you know what is in these reservoirs until you let go and find out? You will discover that what is down there is neither foreign nor scary. With this discovery more trust will emerge, and belief in self will become a tradition.

The Prophecy

The longer I am on this earth, the more aware I become that my attitudes and beliefs are self-fulfilling prophecies: That is, if I believe I can do or be something, chances are I will. If I don't, I won't. It is as simple and as important as that.

For better or for worse, we do become what we think about. If you think about failure long enough, you will eventually become one. These themes are not new but have been echoed throughout history by numerous cultures. How easy it is to forget them and to slip back into the old molds of pessimism and distrust! To be positive and have trust in yourself is hard work. These are essential qualities in any performance formula.

High-level performers have learned the necessity of being positive. They did not inherit positive attitudes, trusts, or beliefs in themselves. Like their skills, these qualities evolved and strengthened by training for them. In their performances as well as in the rest of their lives, they have seen the powers of the self-fulfilling prophecy in action. In the long run, they have learned that it is much easier and more fulfilling to be positive, trust their abilities, and believe in themselves. Their proof is in the performance.

It is a matter of perception. Is the glass half full or half empty? Is it partly sunny or mostly cloudy? The answers to these simple questions are barometers to your attitudes and indicators of the levels of your performances. Either I am *for* myself or I am *against* myself; there are no in-betweens.

Chapter 3 Performance Skills

- In every situation we face and in every decision we make, there are really only two options available to us: to be positive and build ourselves up or to be negative and drag ourselves down. If you do not know which you are doing, you are covertly dragging yourself down.

- It takes more courage, creativity, dedication, and conscious awareness to be positive than to be negative. You have to always actively build yourself up, or you will slip into pessimism.

- It is occasionally appropriate to tear yourself down only if you use it as a means of change or improvement.

- Evaluate your efforts more broadly by reviewing the objectives (end results) as well as the process (means) you employed to reach those ends. Use any evaluation of yourself as a springboard to improvement and refinement.

- You are not out to consciously sabotage your efforts, so believe in yourself.
- Let go of the temptations to monitor every little segment of your performances. Trust that your mind and body know what to do and then let go.
- If you don't know what else to do, be positive!
- Notes: _____

  _____

  _____

  _____

  _____

  _____

- Additions or changes to your personal performance formula:

  _____

  _____

  _____

  _____

  _____

c h a p t e r   4

Charting Your Course to Excellence

Argue for your limitations and, sure enough, they're yours.
—*Richard Bach*

A realistic, positive attitude is a cornerstone for any successful performance. It is the energy that drives and sustains us. However, this energy has to be directed and channeled. Hence, goals and specific plans for reaching those goals are essential for any high-level performance.

We've all been inundated with the importance of establishing goals and plans, but I am still amazed at how few of us take the time to chart our performance courses. Then we wonder why we go off on tangents, flounder, and become discouraged! Establishing and revising goals and plans is another cornerstone for consistently high-level performance.

Goals and plans are important; however, our attitudes about ourselves and our quests are what make a great impact on the actual goals we set. That is, our views of our futures, opportunities, and achievements provide the parameters under which we establish our goals and plans, and we alone determine how narrow or how broad these parameters are.

Limitations and Frontiers

Performers who improve the most are the ones who seem to make a distinction between limitations and something I call frontiers. These people understand that what they achieve is, to a large degree, dependent on their aspirations.

Too often, performers who level off, become distracted, stagnate, or even decline are people who tend to impose limitations on themselves. Many of these people spend inordinate amounts of time, energy, and creativity defending their self-imposed limitations. The following are some of the more common examples of these cop-outs:

- I'll never be able to do that.
- I've never done it before in practice so there is no way I will be able to do it now.
- I can't compete in this weather.
- I never have any luck.
- I never had the right opportunities and chances.
- If only I had good equipment.
- I never received any support.
- I have a stomach ache again.
- The press has always been unfair with me.
- My supervisor won't let me do what I want to do.
- I can't do that because it is my time of the month.
- My biorhythms are all on critical days today!

The danger in focusing on limitations is that after a while, you structure all your efforts in terms of what you cannot do or do only to a point, instead of what you can do or improve upon. Self-imposed limitations are the seeds of frustration, mediocrity, and failure.

Shared Barriers

Very often, limitations expand to many people, and then they all start to believe that no one can do a particular thing. Those of you who are old enough to remember the early 1950s will recall the controversy that revolved around whether the human body could run a mile under 4 minutes. Scientists tried to establish the impossibility of the 4-minute mile. Runners in the late '40s and early '50s would try hard, fail, and further convince themselves that they were at the limits of human functioning. However, it became clear to a very few that the 4-minute mile was, more than anything else, a psychological barrier. One of those who sincerely believed the 4-minute mile could be broken was a young English medical student named Roger Bannister. On a blustery May day in 1954, Bannister broke through this barrier by running a 3:59.4 mile. It was an earth-shattering performance: Not only did it take over a second off the previous world record, but it also shattered all those scientific "proofs" and self-imposed limitations.

Years later, Rainer Martens (R. Martens, personal communication, March 12, 1985) interviewed Sir Roger and found out that during the time of his record-breaking run, Bannister was only running about 30 miles a week—a paultry amount by today's standards. But Bannister had a deep knowledge of what his body could do, and combining this with his medical knowledge of the human body, he convinced himself that he could break the 4-minute barrier. He also realized that this was what he called a "mental barrier." Comforted by this knowledge, he approached the race as a mental challenge rather than as an opportunity to reaffirm the limitations of human beings.

An interesting thing happened during the months following Bannister's performance: No less than six other runners broke 4 minutes, highlighted by John Landy's remarkable 3:58.0. It was as if Sir Roger's run symbolically said to the rest of the milers, "Okay boys, I did it so you can do it too. Now, let's get on with it!"

Pushing the Outside of the Envelope

Bannister's performance not only served as a mold breaker, but it also served as a mold maker. For when a barrier like that is broken, it opens up all sorts of new possibilities. In the book and movie *The Right Stuff*, the test pilots used a marvelous phrase that described their quests of how far beyond the speed of sound they could go. They said, "Let's see how far we can push the outside of the envelope today." For them, there were no demons on the other side of Mach I or Mach II. If anything, these demons were in their self-imposed limitations.

How we approach our performances is a proving ground for our attitudes and beliefs. We can choose to focus on what we can't do and search for reasons why we can't do them, or we can focus on what we can do. As Richard Bach pointed out in the quotation at the beginning of this chapter, as people defend their limitations, all they are really accomplishing is strengthening them.

It is very difficult to allow yourself to excel when you are permeated with self-imposed limitations. Limitations set clear boundaries in the areas of performance. As hard as I might try to improve or extend myself, if I have put up barriers, I then "know" the boundaries of my efforts. Bry (1978) went as far as to say that "The limits of your beliefs define the limits of your realities" (p. 78). Her proposition stems from the self-fulfilling prophecy that I achieve what I define I can achieve; I become what I allow myself to become. Sure, I may not be able to leap tall buildings in a single bound . . . yet! But if I believe there is no way I can ever reach the top of a building, I will never find the stairway.

Limitations are, by definition, limiting. Then what is the alternative? A more productive perspective is to replace the word *limitation* with the word *frontier*. As limitations connote such images of walls and barriers, frontiers connote such images of signposts and measuring sticks; as limitations connote suppression, frontiers connote freedom; as limitations connote a holding back, frontiers connote a letting go; as limitations connote a constricting, frontiers connote an expanding; and as limitations focus on what I cannot do or achieve, frontiers focus on what I eventually do and achieve.

Quite often, people who have good intentions for us try, consciously or not, to impose limitations upon us. Fourteen years ago, I had an operation on my knee. This was back in the orthopedic dark ages when there were few of the advanced techniques and procedures that exist today. After the operation, my surgeon came in and said, "Well, it was a very serious injury. Your rehabilitation will be slow. Probably the best you can ever achieve is to walk *with* a limp." As well intentioned as he was, he was laying a limitation on me. He also said, "During your rehabilitation you will be lifting weights, primarily using the leg extension exercise. Probably the most that knee can ever handle is doing 10 repetitions for three sets with 30 pounds on the bar." Again, another limitation. To this day, I can remember my response. I said to myself, "Now, wait a minute. I am not going to let him tell me how well I can become. After all, he is not in my knee; I am in my knee."

The next day I went down to the rehabilitation clinic to start strengthening my knee. In the beginning, I could barely lift my leg with no added weight. However, with each passing day I improved. Each day I began setting little goals for myself in order to extend myself a bit farther. I amazed the physical therapists by reaching my surgeon's limit exactly 30 days after the operation. That day was not only a big decision-making point in the rehabilitation of my knee, it was also a big decision-making point in the rehabilitation of my mind as well. I said to myself, "I have achieved this in just 30 days. If I believe this is the best condition I can ever attain, I might as well limp right on out of here. No, let's see just what I can accomplish in the next 30 days." Today, I still do the same 10 repetitions for three (or four or five) sets but now with 120 pounds on the bar! I do not walk with a limp; on the contrary, I run all sorts of road races smoothly and rhythmically.

I am sure there are many of you out there who have defied the odds in overcoming adversity. Only you know how far you can go in your life, and the only way you can find out is by doing it. By structuring our efforts based on frontiers rather than limitations, we are giving ourselves permission to extend, to strive, and to eventually excel in all arenas of our lives.

Frontiers create possibilities and opportunities. Frontiers are limitless, or they go as far as we are willing to define them. Each of us have our own performance envelope and only we can determine how far to push its edges.

Goal Setting and Planning

Frontiers establish the framework under which we can create realistic goals and make specific plans for reaching those goals. People who realize more of their potential are those who know where they are going. These people rely on and integrate the processes of goal setting and planning into their daily routines as well as into their performances.

An old saying warns, "If you do not know where you are going, any route will take you there!" Establishing goals—the end results—and plans—the courses to reach those results—provide us with the vision of where we are going. Goals and plans are blueprints or game plans, nothing more. They are jump-off points, but they provide us with the directions with which to proceed.

People often forget that goal setting and planning are important not only in defining performance objectives, but that they are also crucial in developing and reaffirming the senses of mission, purpose, and direction. If we are able to construct goals that relate to our values and priorities, we can increase our commitments to achieving them. When our goals really mean something to us, we can increase and sustain our drives and motivations better than if we just go through the motions. A sense of mission, purpose, and direction is what keeps us on course, especially during the discouraging times. Therefore, one purpose of goal setting is to gain more direction.

When our goals and plans really mean something to our lives, concepts like motivation, drive, ambition, dedication, persistence, and will power become less critical issues. From my experience these concepts have most often become performance issues when goals are not integrated with one's values and priorities. These concepts are then frequently used to externally replace that which is internally missing. If my goals and plans fit in with my values and priorities, my quests become more natural and, in a way, easier to stick with. My missions and purposes are the outward manifestations of my values and priorities; they are the symbolic glue that holds the rest of my performance attributes and qualities together.

The Future

The future can be approached in two major ways: (a) by expectations and (b) by goal setting and planning. Expectations are narrow, rigid ways of approaching the future.

One expects the future to unfold exactly in a prescribed way. Expectations take the forms of "It *must* be this way," "It *should* be easier than this," "I just *have to* do it right now," and "It *ought* to be there." Expectations usually end with such excuses as "If only the wind hadn't blown," "I could have won if the judging were more fair," and "I tried so hard." All these shoulds, coulds, musts, gottas, and oughtas are what Albert Ellis (1973), the famous therapist and author, calls *musterbating.* Musterbating reflects the paradox that the harder I try to rigidly control the future, the less control I have over it.

Dogmatically expecting something to occur in a prescribed way actually inhibits efforts at adjusting or adapting in any form, especially when new information or priorities emerge. People who do this spend all their time worrying about the future or fretting about the past and spend very little time in the here and now. These people do not realize that the only time frame that they can directly influence is the present. "It must be exactly this way and no other way" is the battle cry of the musterbator. Paradoxically, the more they cling to their expectations, especially in the light of new information, the farther away they actually go from meeting their expectations.

A more flexible method of approaching the future is by goal setting and planning. Like other high-performance terms used in this book, *planning* and *goal setting* are important *-ing* terms. Terms ending with *-ing* connote ongoing and changing processes that demand adjusting and adapting. These terms are not ends in themselves; rather they are means to other ends and means.

I have my goals and plans for tonight, for this weekend, and even for next year. However, if new information emerges or my priorities change, I am much more free to alter my plans and goals than if I were bound to my expectations. With this added flexibility I can then adapt and adjust my directions so that my goals remain realistic and appropriate. This flexibility also keeps me open to new possibilities and opportunities as they may emerge— possibilities and opportunities of which I would not be aware if I clung solely to my expectations.

In short, I *use* my goal setting and planning. I am *used by* my expectations. With the greater senses of freedom and flexibility through my goal setting and planning, I will tend to be more creative, effective, and even courageous in exploring my performance frontiers.

The Extremes

Most people approach all types of goal setting in one of two extremes: Either they avoid and neglect it completely, or they become infatuated with it. Many performers mistakenly believe that adding any structure, including goals, to their efforts will disrupt the flow and rhythm of their performances; as a result, they go out of their way to avoid setting goals and making plans. They would much rather "roll with the punches" or "go with the flow." Unfortunately, they usually are swept away and eventually flounder.

These people do not understand that proper goal setting and planning sets the stage for them to attain their best performance rhythms. As they attain better indications of where they are going and what they can achieve, they are actually programming their minds and bodies to accomplish their goals more naturally.

At the other extreme are the musterbater and the people who love planning for planning's sake. These people believe that as they establish precise plans, they will automatically achieve their goals. What they forget, however, is that goal setting and planning are merely blueprints for action and that they must *act* upon these blueprints to reach their goals.

Management By Objectives (MBO) is an excellent case in point. The MBO program was designed to provide measurable direction and criteria for evaluation to business. Unfortunately, many people misinterpreted this to mean that establishing objectives were ends in themselves, so it was not uncommon to find departments that spent 6 months organizing their yearly objectives! Other people threatened by evaluation established goals so low that productivity actually declined. And those who resisted the whole notion of MBO delegated the responsibility of establishing the objectives to one individual while the rest of the personnel went on doing business as usual! Because people saw goal setting and planning as ends in themselves instead of means to better performance and productivity, this good idea was abused.

Appropriate goal setting and planning blends establishing objectives with adjusting to what is occurring during the implementation. This is called the tight-loose property of goal setting. You can specifically plan your actions, but you must be flexible enough to modify these plans as you go along. Top bodybuilders are excellent examples of athletes who live by their goals. They often put in two workouts a day with each workout emphasizing different muscle groups. Within each muscle group are numerous exercises that can be performed to stimulate the muscle from different angles. Long before they ever reach the gym, they have a good idea of the specific types, variations, poundages, and sequences of exercises they will perform during that workout. They may say something like this: "One group I want to work this morning are my pecs (the pectoralis or chest muscles). I will start with five sets of pyramiding bench presses. Then I will do four sets of decline dumbbell bench presses supersetted with weighted dips. Then I will do five sets of incline bench presses. Finally, I will do six sets of flies with some forced repetitions."

However, once they start exercising, they continually monitor how their bodies feel, and they relate this information to their plans for that session. Quite often, they have to alter their routines based on how their bodies feel or what they need. This means either increasing the workout, shortening parts of it, or altering the sequence of the exercises. Top bodybuilders know they always have to adapt. By doing so, they force their muscles to respond in new ways, and this is how muscles grow in size and strength.

At this point you might say, "If I have to always change my goals, what is the point of establishing them at all?" If you did not originally have goals and plans, chances are that you could not see how and where to adapt. Just like pushing a boat off the shore, the very act of setting goals gives us initial direction and impetus. It is then up to us to navigate our performance boats to reach our objectives.

Risking

In its own way, goal setting charts the future. Nothing is absolutely certain when we try to predict the future, so goal setting and planning involve some elements of risk. However, many people are afraid of any kind of risk, for they only see what they may lose from a risk-taking situation. What they do not realize is that taking risks is the only way to improve and extend themselves; therefore, taking risks and personal development go hand in hand.

We forget that we take hundreds of risks every day. We take a risk when we cross the street, ask a question, make a sales call, become vulnerable with a mate, or experiment with a new skill or approach. Most of these situations involve low levels of risk, so we often overlook that they are risks at all. The higher levels of risk, however, are more frightening. Doing a double axle for the first time, going in for an important job interview, taking a law school admission test, performing for an audience, making a presentation, climbing a 5.11 rock, or proposing marriage are examples of higher order risks. It is the fear and dread of these higher order risks that frequently filter down to cloud our views of risk taking in general.

Appropriate risking is an essential component in any effort to extend ourselves. Undoubtedly, risking implies the possibility of failure; however, risking is the only way to see how far we can extend ourselves. There is the possibility of loss, but there is also the opportunity for great gains. The trick is to know which risks are appropriate and contain the best chances for success.

As in many other areas of high-level performance, the wisdom of determining which are appropriate risks evolves from experience with similar situations. Brendan Liddell, a former philosophy professor of mine, was fond of saying, "Good judgments come from experience and experience comes from bad judgments." Experience is a necessary—albeit sometimes painful—teacher for assessing appropriate risks.

Elite and creative performers who push the edges of their personal envelopes realize that in these new performance frontiers everything is a risk. Everything is new and unfamiliar. These people have learned to cope and even have become comfortable functioning with ambiguity, uncertainty, and insecurity. They know that the best way to capitalize on their frontiers is to implicitly trust that they are doing the right things as well as they can. Belief in self is the only security.

The prologue of the old television series *Star Trek* included this phrase: ". . . to boldly go where no man has gone before." Shaping your views of the future in terms of frontiers is the map to use to see just how far you can go. How to chart this map will be explored in the next chapter.

Chapter 4 Performance Skills

- You choose how to approach your future. Define your performances and yourself in terms of frontiers (what you can do) instead of your limitations (what you cannot do).

- Goal setting and planning are essential tools to excellence. No one can do without them. Properly done, they provide both the structure and flexibility needed to extend performance frontiers.

- Rigid expectations or the more flexible processes of goal setting and planning are the two basic ways to approach the future. There are no ends to goal setting and planning; each achievement signals a new beginning.

- Do not become wrapped up in establishing goals and plans for their own sake. They are meant to be used. Employ your goals and plans as springboards to action.

- Living is a risk. Focus on what you may gain from a risk-taking situation instead of what you may lose. Learn to accept risk taking as part of the process of extending your performance frontiers.

- Notes: _____

_____

_____

_____

_____

_____

- Additions or changes to your personal performance formula:

  _____

  _____

  _____

  _____

  _____

chapter 5

The Goal-Setting Program

Great minds have purposes, others have wishes.
—Washington Irving

No matter your sport, activity, business, or performance specialty, any use of effective goal setting and planning must include some essential elements. This chapter will explore the key elements in any process of practical goal setting and planning. In order to really maximize this chapter, take your time in filling out all the questions. This is the best way to assure you of developing your own goal-setting program.

Assessment

Goal setting and planning are really not all that difficult. All they require is a little time and a great deal of honesty. Before you can determine where you want to go, you have to recognize where you are now. Therefore, an accurate assessment of you and your skill level is an essential starting point.

Answer the following questions either here or in your performance journal. In your performance specialty,

• Where are you in your overall progress right now?

_____

_____

- What are your strengths?

  _____

  _____

- What do you specifically need to improve?

  _____

  _____

- What things have you improved?

  _____

  _____

- In a performing or competitive situation, what things do you need to do well, or better, in order to excel?

  _____

  _____

Any assessment of one's current status must be done fairly and objectively. However, many people assess themselves in very counterproductive ways. Some judge themselves harshly, focusing only on those aspects they do poorly. Other people lie or delude themselves, pretending to be better than they really are. Still others constantly compare themselves to other performers by setting themselves up and always coming up short.

An honest assessment of yourself is meant to provide a base of information and understanding from which you can build upon your strengths and improve on your weaknesses. Assessing is a realistic and objective review (literally, "re-view") of yourself. The only time frame we have control over is the here and now, and assessing ourselves is meant to ground us more in the present. The clearer view we have of ourselves and the better we accept this view, the more we can control ourselves and fashion our individual courses to excellence.

Meaning

Any assessment of yourself should include determining precisely what your activity or pursuit means to you. Ask yourself the following questions:

• What value or priority do you place on your activity?

_____

_____

• What personal needs are met by your doing this?

_____

_____

• How does this activity fit in with the rest of your life?

_____

_____

• What personal sacrifices have you made to pursue this activity?

_____

_____

• Have these sacrifices been worth it? _____

• Could you see your life without this activity? _____

• Do you genuinely enjoy this activity for its own sake?

_____

• How do you feel about yourself when you do it?

_____

_____

Such questions are designed to assess the deeper meanings of your performance activity. As you begin to understand what your activity means to you, you will notice an increase in your direction, purpose, and motivation for your pursuit.

Motivation is one of the most overused and least understood concepts in sports, business, and the performing arts. Too often, it is used as a general catchall excuse for poor efforts. In some circles, motivation has taken on even some magical and mystical connotations, which only serve to keep the concept confused, unclear, and impractical.

Motivation is really not that hard of a concept to understand and to apply. The best way to do this is to break down the word itself. Ask yourself this: What are my *motives* in my performance activity?

You can break this down even further to assess exactly what your *needs* and *wants* are in your activity. As you gain a clearer understanding of the meanings of your pursuits, you will better be able to see that motivation is an outward manifestation of these meanings; and as you achieve this realization, the less of a problem and more of an ally motivation will be for you.

Understanding the meanings of your activity is the core of your quest for performing excellence. From this center you can then employ such qualities as motivation, mission, and purpose.

Dreams and Aspirations

As I understand and accept my attributes and the meanings behind my performance activity, I also need to put them in perspective with my dreams and aspirations. Any comprehensive assessment must include the here-and-now views of me as well as the long-term views of my dreams and aspirations.

Dreaming and aspiring are such neglected processes in goal setting. They can provide us with tremendous amounts of desire, direction, and perspective. Now, allow your mind to wander while asking yourself the following questions:

• What would I like to eventually achieve in my performance specialty?

_____

_____

• How far can I take this?   _____

• How would I feel excelling in my activity? (Be specific.)

_____

_____

• Who do I aspire to be most like?   _____

• What kinds of opportunities would open up for me when I become the performer of my dreams?

_____

_____

• What would I do when I achieve my dreams?

_____

_____

In this rational and analytical world, we often overlook the powers of dreaming and aspiring. These processes open us up to new possibilities, options, and frontiers. They also give us back the childlike qualities of awe and wonder from which we can gain the vision and the desire to go after our dreams.

Our dreams and aspirations are the metaphorical rocks of our goals. Our honest assessments of our abilities and the meanings behind our pursuits are the metaphorical chisels of our goals. Together, they enable us to start carving out a wonderful and precise sculpture of our performance goals and plans.

Specificity

From the base of the information gained from our assessments, we are now in a position to devise our performance goals and plans. It should come as no surprise to the reader that a key ingredient is specificity. The more specific we make our goals and plans, the clearer pictures we create in directing our actions.

Appropriate and Attainable

The two major components of specific goal setting and planning are appropriateness and attainability. Too often, novices and mediocre performers set such vague, unrealistic, or grandiose goals (if they set them at all) that they are unlikely to be met. Whenever you structure your plans on an all-or-nothing basis, most often the result will be nothing.

The establishment of effective goals is like a ladder. The appropriateness of the goals is like the frame of the ladder that is always parallel and continuous. The attainability of the goals is like the rungs of a ladder that are spaced close enough together to enable a smooth climb, yet far enough apart to present a challenge.

Consistently high-level performers know that in order to reach their ultimate objectives, they have to establish a series of intermediate goals. They know that with the attainment of a goal comes a sense of closure and that they gain momentum to be used as a springboard to the next goal. By setting attainable goals, they allow themselves the opportunity to feel that they have achieved something. This little step also reminds them of their long-term directions and pursuits. For example, a good salesperson may plan to make 10 cold calls on a given day. A mediocre salesperson may plan cold calls using such words as *some, a bunch,* or *as many as I can.* Good salespeople know that by making more specific plans, they more often attain their goals as well as gain the incentives to continue.

Elite performers seem to possess an interesting perspective in their goal attainments. At any moment during their training or working, they believe that they are in the process of attaining their goals. Even if the performance is months away, these performers believe that they are right now in the process of succeeding or performing well. For example, a figure skater might be thinking, "I am now in the process of skating beautifully in next week's competition"; a good salesperson might believe, "I am now in the process of closing this sale"; a lawyer might reaffirm, "I am now in the process of passing next month's bar examination"; a dancer might remind herself, "I am now in the process of dancing wonderfully in tomorrow's ballet"; or a supervisor might tell himself, "My department is now in the process of meeting this quarter's quotas."

Much of the performance anxiety we experience emanates from the belief that we have just one short chance to perform well. Changing perspectives to broaden the process of performing does much to lessen this anxiety. If I believe that I am currently in the process of succeeding at next month's competition, I will likely experience less pressure because I have expanded my definition of what that performance entails to include all my practices, rehearsals, and preparations.

By setting appropriate and attainable goals, performers soon discover that they can meet their goals not just once, but consistently. They then can see concrete progress. This progress produces a higher degree of confidence, and this increase in confidence fuels the momentum to aspire and to reach for higher rungs of their performance ladders.

Performance Goals

Establishing goals over which you have control is as important as appropriate and attainable goals setting and planning. Good performers give greater emphasis to creating performance goals as opposed to outcome goals. Frequently, we do not have total control over the outcomes of our efforts. Conditions may change, another competitor may have a peak performance, teammates may make critical errors, there may be questionable judging, or the buyer may have other needs and priorities. Therefore, establish goals such as, "I will emphasize my follow-through today," or "I will be really positive and eager," instead of "We will win today," "I will shoot a 69 in this round of golf," or "I will get this account."

Establish your goals and plans around what you need to do to perform well today instead of what you need to do to win or to be a success. It is a subtle distinction, but a very important one. Focus on doing those things over which you have the greatest degree of control. Chances are that you will succeed more frequently, but even if you don't, you will have the satisfaction of knowing you gave it your best.

As you establish your performance goals, spend a little time thinking about options and contingency plans that you could adopt in the course of your performance if your original goals become inappropriate or unattainable. Remember, top performers exhibit both of the qualities of establishing specific goals as well as having the flexibility to adapt and adjust. Don't dwell on alternatives, for then you won't give your best shot to your original plans. Rather, ponder your contingencies something like this: "If my original game plan isn't working, I will do this or this." Stay flexible to create new plans so your efforts remain appropriate and attainable to the performance situation you are in at any one point in time.

Make your goals and plans for reaching those goals as specific as possible. The more specific your goals and the more focused your individual performance plans, the less you will leave to chance and the more overall control you will have in reacing these goals. Remember, you are the captain of your performance ship, and as such, only you determine *where* you are going and *how* you are going to get there.

Time Lines and Performance Cycles

Although I have encouraged establishing specific short-term performance goals, it is important to keep your long-term plans in perspective. Many performers become so wrapped up in their short-range objectives that they lose sight of their long-range goals. For this reason, an increasing number of performers are regularly employing time lines and performance cycles.

Time Lines

Time lines are simple and effective tools to organize and to plot your course to a major goal. Think now of a major goal you have in the future. It could be an athletic event, a test, a sales quota, or a premiere. Specify this goal on the time line in Figure 5.1 together with its completion date. Next, plot out all the specific subgoals, sequences, and desired dates of accomplishment along this line. You will see in Figure 5.1 that some goal lines are longer than others; this is because some subgoals (e.g., having similar experiences) are more essential than others (e.g., making travel arrangements). You will also notice that some of these subgoals are grouped closer together than others; this is because progress is rarely linear and because some goals must be met in a specific sequence (e.g., learning how to ask questions before learning how to close a sale).

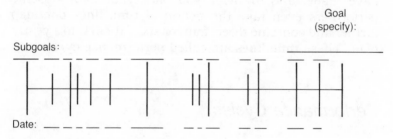

Figure 5.1   Time line to goal completion.

As you organize your time lines, include not only the skills and experiences you wish to attain, but also the attitudes you wish to emphasize as well as the logistical considerations. In the process of achieving your subgoals, frequently refer back to your time line. Feel free to modify it, either by adding, deleting, or combining subgoals or by changing their sequences and completion dates. For example, if I want to reach my sales quota for a given quarter, my time line might look like the one in Figure 5.2.

Writing out your goals and putting them on a time line makes them seem easier to accomplish. Using a time line (a) gives you a better sense of control, organization, and direction, (b) promotes greater commitment to your goals, (c) helps relieve worry and confusion, especially as perfor-

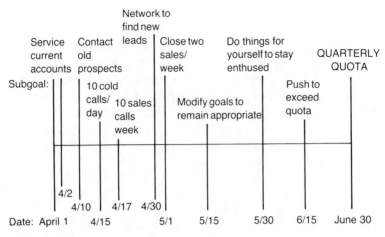

Figure 5.2 Sample time line to reach quarterly sales quota.

mance time approaches, by illustrating the progress you have made, and (d) helps you pace your efforts. Some performers even take the notion of time lines one step further and combine three, four, or six of them into a yearly plan. These time lines are called performance cycles.

Performance Cycles

Top performers realize that they can only give a few maximal efforts within a year. Flat, inconsistent performances will result if they attempt too many. They must give themselves enough time to rest and recuperate, to learn new skills and/or techniques, and to pace themselves.

Performance cycles include time lines, but they also include low-intensity and rest times as well. A typical performance cycle usually begins by starting with low-intensity activities, by changing bad habits, and by learning new major skills (see Figure 5.3).

For example, a female runner who is planning her next calendar year will start off plotting the times she wishes to give maximal efforts. These could be the indoor championships, outdoor college championships, world track and field championships, and the Olympic Games. In the first cycle she might emphasize bodybuilding or long-endurance training to build up her deficiencies, culminating in some

Figure 5.3   Typical performance cycle.

indoor races. For her college championships she might emphasize relay events or different distances in order to help out her team. Then in the summer, she might go to Europe to run several big races. After some recuperation time, she might establish cycles working toward the Olympic trials and the Games themselves. With all these demands, you can see why she has to plan a whole year in advance.

Whether an athlete, a dancer, or a salesperson, an increasing amount of performers are using personal logs and journals to record their training, impressions, insights, emphases, and plans. Especially at elite levels, lives become so fast and complex that people cannot expect themselves to remember every detail of their training or performing. Thus, many keep meticulous notes monitoring their progression through their time lines and performance cycles. Keeping such a log relieves much of the stress of trying to remember every little thing and is an indispensable tool for charting progress. Time lines and performance cycles are excellent methods of keeping track of your long-range goals. Having these goals organized in such ways will better enable you to retain the perspectives necessary to establish appropriate and attainable short-range goals.

Don Hutson, a top professional speaker, has said that there are no unrealistic goals, oniy unrealistic time lines. I don't know if I would go quite that far, but I do know the only way to find out what is realistic is to plan, proceed, ponder, and plan again. In this sense, your goals and plans are your springboards from which you can dive into the waters of becoming the best possible you.

Prioritizing

A much overlooked element of goal setting and planning is prioritizing. Most mediocre and inconsistent performers categorize their priorities in two extremes—either everything is important or nothing is. These people usually have not developed the abilities to discriminate the relative importance of goals, actions, sequences, and commitments.

Priorities are those decisions we deem more important to attaining our goals; therefore, we commit a greater degree of time and energy to them. Our priorities should reflect our values, missions, and purposes. If they do not, a performer is destined to fail.

If any one quality distinguishes elite performers from their good colleagues, it is their ability to prioritize. Elite performers have tunnel vision when it comes to following their priorities. Because they know what is important, they will not be diverted from their priorities.

There is a metaphysical proverb that goes, "Once you make up your mind, you literally make up your mind." Prioritizing sets all those inner mental and physical wheels in motion that effectively channel the performers' efforts into achieving their goals. Dedication, perseverance, commitment, drive, and intensity all stem from this ability to set priorities.

It is one thing to set priorities, it is quite another thing to live with their implications. Many people are not aware that these are two separate processes. Surely, you must know someone who is famous for making promises and commitments but who never follows through on them. I have a colleague whom we call "No Problem Johnson." He always says "no problem" as he commits himself to something, but that is usually the last thing we ever hear from him! Productive people and effective performers alike have learned that it is as important to follow through on their priorities as it is to establish them.

Saying No

I have only a limited amount of time and energy. Prioritizing implies that there will be some issues in my life that will have to take a back seat for a while. Few of us like rejection, whether giving or receiving it. That is why it is so hard for many of us to say no. The ability to say no is the most difficult skill to learn in living with our priorities. Most coaches and teachers have known cases of performers who achieve some measure of initial success and receive a great variety of offers and opportunities and cannot say no to any of them. Their performances soon suffer and they usually lose the perspective of what made them successful in the first place.

It took me a long time to realize that by honestly saying no to some offer or request, I was really saying yes to my commitments and priorities. People who have learned to live with their priorities know that opportunities will always come along and that the best way to take care of themselves is to stick with their decisions and commitments. In this respect, saying no is really an affirmation of self. Therefore, continually assess your priorities. Realize that you cannot do everything at once or be all things to all people. When you establish your goals and plans, recognize that only you have control and responsibility over the sequences and directions of your efforts.

Juggling Your Life

As with any other goal, priorities are not permanent. New ones must intermittently be established. In order to maintain a balance in my performing, as well as in the rest of my life, those issues that took a back seat must eventually be given a priority. Those selfish individuals who constantly prioritize the same things at the expense of other areas of their lives will soon end up discouraged, burned out, unhappy, or lonely.

High-level performers know that there is a time to put out and a time to recoup. In this respect, goal setting and planning must also be seen in the larger framework of balancing an entire life. The whole interchange of planning, prioritizing, and balancing is like juggling. I love to juggle. I almost flunked out of my first semester in college when everyone on my dormitory floor was learning to juggle! There is something fascinating about physically coordinating three or more objects. There is also something challenging about the dynamics of concentrating on juggling.

We can apply the metaphor of juggling into our lifestyles. For example, I have four balls and each represents a major area of my life (e.g., career/performance, health, family, and spiritual). Juggling these balls, my goal is to maintain a fluid rhythm among them. At any one time, only one ball is in my hand. This is the only ball (area of my life) over which I have any direct control and, as such, must give it priority. If I keep it in my hand too long (i.e., give it too much attention), the other balls will get out of synch, collide, and fall to the ground. On the other hand (sorry!), if I don't give the ball in my hand enough attention (i.e., avoid it), I will again lose my overall rhythm, and the other balls will come crashing to the ground.

Other corollaries to this metaphor of juggling your life are as follows:

- If you change the time a ball is in your hand, you must also change the height and pace of the other balls.

- If you add or subtract a ball, you must also change the entire rhythm of the rest.

- Because there is an optimal height in juggling, the best way to find it is to experience the effects of tossing the balls too high and too low.

- Because tenseness causes poor catches and inconsistent tosses, you must relax.

- You must learn how to pay singular attention to the ball in your hand and remain totally aware of all the balls simultaneously.

- There are always adjustments to make.

- If you drop a ball or the balls collide in the air, they will always go to opposite ends of the room, roll under couches, or lodge in between immovable objects!

Effective performers are known for their single-mindedness. However, elite performers, especially those who endure over time, are not only known for their prioritizing, but also for their abilities to shift gears and to juggle their lives. Effective juggling of life roles is dependent on the interplay of adequately addressing each one while keeping them all in a coordinated rhythm. When achieved, the benefits of the rhythmical juggling of one's life is far greater than the sum of the individual parts. This is the foundation on which many sustaining elite performers rely.

Monitoring

Any goal setting or planning implies that there must be continual monitoring to assess whether the goals are still appropriate, attainable, and what adjustments (if any) are to be made. In this sense, assessing and monitoring interconnect to form an ongoing cycle. Many times, you will find that your goals have become inappropriate or unattainable. Continual monitoring of your progress is beneficial in that it detects the incongruencies earlier, so you waste less time moving in counterproductive directions.

Monitoring forces you to occasionally reevaluate yourself and/or your goals. When doing so, gather as much feedback from as many sources as possible (i.e., performance results, time lines, logs or journals, supervisors, coaches, family, and friends). Use all of this feedback to decide if you are on course or if you need to chart out a new one. Even if you decide that you are still on course, the process of monitoring is valuable because it gives you an opportunity to reaffirm your goals and plans as well as the incentive to continue.

Do not be afraid to monitor your progress. Recognize this as essential in reaching your goals. Monitoring is your insurance policy that will help keep you moving toward attaining your performance goals.

Goal setting, planning, time lines, performance cycles, prioritizing, juggling, and monitoring can be seen as a continuous spiral that leads to ever-increasing levels of performance excellence. In some part of your consciousness you are always planning, pondering, deciding. So it is easy to take these processes one step further and more consciously structure your goals and plans. When you do this, I think you will be amazed at how much control you will feel and at what you can accomplish.

Chapter 5 Performance Skills

- A goal-setting program must include an honest assessment of your present status, motives, purposes, dreams, and aspirations.

- Make your goals and plans as specific and detailed as possible. Structure your goals so that they are appropriate and attainable. Formulate specific performance goals instead of vague outcome goals.

- Time lines and performance cycles are helpful tools in plotting out subgoals, dates of achievement, and sequences. These tools help organize your quests and keep you more in charge of your progress.

- Keep your major goals in perspective by prioritizing them. It is one thing to establish goals, make decisions, or give commitments; it is quite another thing to live with them. Keep your life priorities in balance by learning how to "juggle" your lifestyle.

- Continually monitor your progress using as many sources of feedback as possible. Feel free to adjust your goals and plans so they become even more appropriate and attainable.

- List your short-range goals for the next 2 weeks:

  To _____

  To _____

  To _____

  To _____

- Notes: _____

  _____

  _____

  _____

  _____

  _____

- Additions or changes to your personal performance formula:

  _____

  _____

  _____

  _____

  _____

chapter 6

Nothing to Fear But . . .

He who is afraid of a thing gives it power over him.
—Moroccan Proverb

One of the greatest inhibitors of maximizing our potentials and of improving our performances is fear. Perhaps it may seem a little incongruent to talk about such a negative topic after I have been so positive in the last few chapters; however, before we can maximize performance, we must minimize detractors, and fear is one of the most serious performance detractors.

Most of us have experienced fear in our performances. Some of us even have been paralyzed by it, and a few of us live with it daily. Franklin Roosevelt's "There is nothing to fear but fear itself" is valid to a point. However, fears can take on some very real forms within us. There is no result of fear more obvious than that demonstrated in performing. Understanding and overcoming our performance fears are crucial if we are to continually expand our performance frontiers and to achieve our goals.

Fear is common. We all occasionally become afraid. You are not the only one who has ever been afraid before or during a performance. On the contrary, those performers who brag that they have never been afraid are the ones who are usually hiding something. Referring to one of his plays, William Inge (1957) said, "It has taken me many years of living to realize the fears in all of us, the fears in the most seemingly brave, the bravery in the most seemingly frightened" (p. 57). Many fears are fraught with misconceptions and even deeper fears. We have to go past these notions in order to discover how our fears specifically affect our performance.

If they had personalities of their own, fears should be complimented for their ingenuity and shrewdness in how they creep into us. When more obvious explanations for a poor performance are discarded, quite often some kind of fear was responsible. Beyond that, when the more obvious forms of fear are stripped away, it is amazing how often a more subtle and devious fear is at the root of the problem. For example, many businessmen fear speaking before large groups. In some instances further investigation might provide more in-depth information. The speaker may actually fear rejection and interpret it as commentary on his or her value as a person. Fears, like a virus, can quickly become pervasive and influence every part of our lives.

Although we have fears unique to each of us, performers do share some similar kinds of fears. Five major categories of fears, each having a number of subcategories, affect our performances. Let's begin by examining the most common fear.

Failure and Success

Two of the most prevalent fears among performers are the fears of failure and success. On the surface, these two fears seem to be dissimilar; however, they are quite interrelated. It is not so much a matter of which of these two fears a performer has as it is the combination of both.

Most of us can remember childhood performances where we were so afraid of failing that we had sleepless nights or actually became sick before the performance. At that age, those fears were not so much of failing as they were of performing itself or of letting down our parents, teachers, and friends.

As we matured so did our fears of failure. As pressures to succeed and to excel increased, the possibilities of failure became more apparent. During those years a failure in an event was intertwined with our whole self-image. We equated any failure in a situation with the judgment that we were failures as individuals as well. These were very scary times, for we were always on guard for what we might lose—not only from a performance, but from our self-images as well.

When we allow the fear of failure to take hold of us, we usually imagine all the disastrous things that could possibly destroy a good performance. Rain, unfair judging, the set falling down, mistakes by teammates, missed travel connections, the microphone or tape system malfunctioning, or the mind becoming a total blank are common fantasies. Fears of failure then set our minds churning on all the possible negative consequences of the failure. We fantasize about such things as rejection, ridicule, embarrassment, demotion, lost opportunities, or about letting down someone else. So even before the performance, those who have fears of failure are already rehearsing how they are going to react when they fail!

As with so many other instances of poor performances, the more we focus on our fears of failure, the more we actually ensure failure. The more we think about what might go wrong or the consequences of a failure, the greater chances we have of becoming anxious or sick, of freezing or choking, or of just giving a flat performance. Even when our fears of failure are not that paralyzing, the more we allow our fears to govern us, the less we are able to give our best efforts. When fears of failure permeate our thinking, we are apt to hold something back from our performance and believe that "if I am going to fail anyway, why should I put everything on the line?" When we approach our performances with such mind-sets, we are destined to be disappointed.

It is a very rare person who can use a fear of failure productively. A young Jimmy Connors had such an intense fear of failure that he would use this fear to spur him on to victory when on the verge of defeat. Losing was so appalling to him that he would make herculean efforts to avoid it. Luciano Pavarotti constantly fears failure and uses this fear to shock him out of any feelings of complacency. Barry Manilow was racked with doubts and fears early in his career but used them to drive himself harder to succeed. Some entrepreneurs so fear the possibility of having to return to a 9-to-5 job that they spur themselves onward to success. These are very rare examples, however. Given the same circumstances, most of us would allow these fears to rule us.

Those who have fears of failure often feel trapped. Not only do they possess that fear, but they also have the secondary fear that they will never be able to do anything about it. So these fears establish a spiraling, vicious cycle.

The fears of failure inhibit best efforts, thus contributing to poor performances. These poor results promote more doubts and greater fears of failure. As this cycle deepens, performers begin to feel hopeless in believing this pattern will be unchanging. They feel increasingly trapped and start searching for any way out, even going as far as quitting their performance specialty. Although they may resign from that arena, the scars, nevertheless, remain.

Even though a fear of failure is devastating, it must be seen in perspective with its counterpart. This relative of the fear of failure accounts for a greater percentage of poor and inconsistent performances than many of us are aware. More covert and devious than the fear of failure is the fear of success.

On the surface, everyone aspires for success. But let's dig deeper. What would happen if all your performance dreams and aspirations came true? Initially, you would respond with feelings of joy and satisfaction. But what about after that? If you performed spectacularly once, you would probably experience pressure (external and internal) to perform that way, or even better, the next time. If you became a professional or Olympic athlete, a prima ballerina, a junior vice-president, or a virtuoso, wouldn't you also be more accountable to an increasing number of people, live a more complicated life, give up much more of your privacy, and even lose touch with your roots and perspectives?

Success can be a very frightening thing. Maslow (1971) called the fear of success "The Jonah Complex," which was derived from the biblical story of Jonah attempting to run away from his fate. Maslow said that this complex represented the "fears of one's own greatness, the evasion of one's destiny, or the running away from one's own best talents" (p. 35). With the prospects of success or victory at hand, performers who fear success often prefer to sabotage their efforts (frequently subconsciously) and choose mediocrity or even failure. They perceive comfort and acceptance in mediocrity in that they feel they will not stand out from the crowd so much. They often conclude that failure would seem much easier to live with than success. Even for those who do not experience such degrees of fear of success, there are many more who covertly fear recognition, compliments, and attention. There is still another group of people who fear success because they are unwilling to totally commit themselves to excellence. Yet, within all of these people remains the nagging feeling that they somehow betrayed themselves or cut themselves apart.

The fears of failure and success can be extremely covert, too. Up through my college years, I took an unusual sort of pride in my sport injuries. I felt a kind of masochistic satisfaction in being the most injured player on my college soccer team. I would valiantly (but poorly) "play with pain," or better yet, not play at all. "If only I didn't have this bad ankle" was my battle cry. I perceived my injuries as badges of honor—examples of my efforts. In reality, my injuries were convenient excuses for my inability to perform well. You see, it was much easier to try hard and to become injured than to put all my eggs in one basket and risk losing—and possibly winning. Somewhere I intuitively knew that if I really performed well and I was successful, more demands would be made upon me to repeat the performance. If that happened, I feared my inherent fears of failure would be intensified, and with the inevitable failure, my world would come crashing down around me.

Even though I wasn't fully aware of it at the time, my injuries were convenient excuses. My well-intentioned effort was sabotaged by my fears. On the exterior, I was dedicated and noble, but inside I was afraid and ashamed. The fears of failure and success are fraternally enmeshed with each other. One or the other of these fears may be more prevalent at certain times, but if one is present, then the other is not far behind. These fears inhibit most performers to varying degrees during different points in their careers. Subtlety is the major power of these fears, for they are disguised in covert and devious forms. A great deal of conscious awareness is necessary to understand and to eventually overcome these two fears.

The fears of failure and success can be effectively combatted with consistent and effective goal setting. Beginning to view performance, *not* the outcome, as the unit of evaluation allows you to approach the possibility of numerous, smaller successes. These successes, rather than acting as breeding grounds for fears, will provide the bases for more productive self-evaluation. Such a procedure will allow performances to be viewed not as a final end, but as the means to better results. Thus, fear of failure or success will be minimized by having reduced the importance of the performance by focusing on a task rather than on the outcome.

None of us consciously likes to fail, but very few of us are willing to do whatever it takes to succeed. Hence, we join the great masses of mediocrity. Although the fears of failure and success are the most prominent among performers, they are by no means the only ones.

Rejection

Closely related to the fears of failure and success is a group of fears broadly categorized under the fear of rejection. These fears include not only rejection, but also the fears of taking risks, of being embarrassed, ridiculed, and of being discovered as a fraud.

Performing is a risk in itself. Performers often feel very much alone when performing. Even in team, department, or troupe efforts, all performers come face to face with their own abilities and their own alonenesses. By extending themselves in their efforts and through the concurrent feelings of aloneness, many performers feel vulnerable. This vulnerability is increased when the performers know they will be evaluated, judged, rated, or critiqued.

No one likes being rejected, but evaluation of performances are often seen as expressions of rejection. What frequently stands out in performers' and judges' minds is not so much what was done well, but what was done poorly. For many, to criticize is easier than to compliment. To develop the kind of "thick skin" necessary to interpret evaluations and learn from them takes much experience. Even then it is still sometimes hard not to feel rejected.

Mistakes are inevitable when performers risk and extend themselves. The prospects of embarrassment resulting from such mistakes, as well as the perceived ridicule associated with them, are more than some performers can handle. Hence, the more these performers fear mistakes, the less likely they are to extend themselves— and the less they extend themselves, the poorer their performances become.

Fears of rejection and embarrassment often take huge proportions, especially when performers' lives are out of balance to the extend that they believe their performing is the only thing of value. In such circumstances these performers believe in the adolescent notion that every little practice or performance is a test not only of their abilities, but also is an indication of their overall worth as persons. When their lives are skewed in such ways, these performers will always be very sensitive to any perceived rejection and ridicule. Even worse, this perceived rejection is often blown out of proportion. These people frequently conclude that they are not only worthless as performers, but extrapolate their rejection to include a rejection of themselves as individuals.

Related to these fears is the fear of discovery. This fear emanates from the performer's irrational belief that he or she is really a fraud. These performers often feel they don't deserve their accomplishments because they do not possess realistic, positive attitudes and wholehearted trust in themselves. Believing they are fooling everyone and are living a lie, they are convinced that they don't really have any talent and that it will only be a matter of time before they are discovered and exposed. This fear of being discovered as a fraud is then compounded with the fears of the embarrassment, ridicule, and rejection they believe will follow. As a result, these performers begin to live very secret, defensive, and sad lives.

For performers who have these fears, everything becomes a struggle. They spend so much effort protecting themselves that their performances invariably suffer. They are then left only with their fears.

The possibility of failure, rejection, or embarrassment in any performing situation always exists. High-level performers, however, have learned to focus on what is probable instead of what is possible. Sure, there is a small chance that they will be rejected or embarrassed, but there is a much greater chance that they will perform well and succeed. They learn to embrace risks as opportunities to grow. As the old Chinese proverb goes, ''The greatest risk in the world is to risk nothing.'' Cross those bridges of rejection, ridicule, embarrassment, and discovery if and when you come to them. Keeping performance specialties in perspective and realizing that they are only one facet of our lives provides us a way to cross the stream of rejection. Failure to sign an account, land a part, or make a team does not signal character fault or a rejection of the individual, but rather simply signals a minor setback in a performance specialty.

Change

The third category of fear is the fear of change. Any change involves a measure of uncertainty. Those who fear change are afraid because (a) they know that they cannot control the uncertainty, (b) they fear any kind of risking, tending to always focus on what they may lose, and (c) they would rather stay within their shells of security.

Especially with marginally successful performers and coaches, this fear may be exacerbated by the doubt, "Why should I tamper with what used to be successful?" Although there is wisdom in the maxim that "One should never change a winning game," there usually comes a time when once successful strategies are no longer appropriate. It is then counterproductive to try and cling to the old ways.

Many of us hold on to outdated or outmoded beliefs and strategies simply because they represent familiarity, stability, or security. Those of you who have experienced an unhappy, personal relationship can attest to that. During those times you might have said to yourself, "I know he is an insensitive and uncaring idiot, but he is a *familiar* insensitive and uncaring idiot!"

This mind-set is like holding on to a rock in the middle of a river. It may not be the best place in the world, but at least it represents some form of security, stability, and familiarity. The problem with this strategy is that eventually other debris starts to snag on you, drag you down even farther, and make it impossible to ever let go.

During the last decade, "burn out" has been a popular concept. It represented living a life that was too stressful and hectic. Now the latest offshoot of the classic concept of burn out is "rust out." Most of us know individuals who are so reluctant to change and adapt that they seem to be rusting away. It is not the overt pressure that drags them down, but their unwillingness to adapt and adjust. "Nothing surprises me anymore," "If it was good 20 years ago, it should be good now," and "I've earned my taking-it-easy," are the mottos of these people. These kind of people are often caught in security traps. They may be miserable, but they are afraid to let go and flow with their personal or career rivers. Thus, they sit, refusing to change, trying desperately to cope, and slowly rust out.

It takes a great deal of awareness to realize when long-proven strategies or beliefs are no longer appropriate or productive. After that awareness, it takes an even greater deal of trust and courage to let go of them, especially when no alternatives are immediately in sight. Referring back to the river analogy, it takes a strong belief in self to let go of that rock and to flow with the river. Only then will you be able to see alternatives downstream that were not visible from the rock.

Using another analogy, those of you who are familiar with sailing know that it is much more difficult to maneuver the boat when it is dead in the water as opposed to when it is under way. Even if you are going in the wrong direction, you can use this momentum to put you on the right course. Those who refuse to get under way because the wind isn't right will not go anywhere.

Change is essential to all improvement in performing. Those of you who are unwilling to untie yourselves from the dock of security will never see the sunset from the middle of the lake. Allow yourself to experience change as a new opportunity, a challenge. Change is not always negative, nor is it always a test of your ability. As the winds of change batter your sailboat of performance, tack as necessary and sail your way into the safe harbor of performing your best.

Discomfort

When observing high school football practices, I am always amused to see how the coaches push and exhort their players, while the players seem to hold back for fear of injury or discomfort. It is a marvelous set of dynamics to observe. As the coach yells, "Try harder," "Bear down," or

"Get tough," the players seem to ease off even further, and then the coach usually pulls out his or her hair!

While the fear of injury is quite an appropriate response in training situations, the fear of discomfort really only serves to retard improvement. Part of any exploration of performance frontiers entails learning how to overcome the fear of discomfort. Discomfort is a concrete indication that one is pushing both mind and body into new levels of functioning. As the mind and body adjust to these new levels, the discomfort will disappear, and a higher base of functioning will emerge.

Very often we have to shock ourselves out of the complacency of functioning and performing at accustomed levels in order to improve. More and more people who exercise have learned to actually look forward to the discomfort. They know that then, and only then, are they pushing and extending themselves. Discomfort is an inner gauge they use to indicate that they are extending themselves into new frontiers of development and performance.

There is a fine line between discomfort and actual injury. It takes experience and awareness to know where one's fine line is and just how far to push during practice. Those who claim they don't have any fear of injury are usually hiding something, perhaps even from themselves. While the fear of injury is a valid response, many use this as a smoke screen to hide their fears of discomfort, success, and risk.

Discomfort is as much mental as it is physical. The body can often endure much more than the mind thinks it can. Even in such exhausting efforts as a marathon, a cross-country bicycle race, or in the 15th round of a boxing match, it is the mind that often gives up first. Mental discomfort is more covert and subtle than physical discomfort. Where the body gives very direct signals, the mind says, "We don't really have to do that last exercise today," "We don't have the time right now," "I'll call her tomorrow," and "Oh, that shower will feel so good!" Overcoming the specific fear of mental discomfort is essential in order to give the body a chance to discover just how far it can go.

Getting used to discomfort is necessary for improvement in any performance specialty. As in building a muscle, we must first exhaust the outer and more frequently used fibers of our performance selves before we can stimulate the inner and untapped fibers. As we reach down to these inner layers of our performance selves and cope with the discomfort, new standards of excellence will emerge.

Fearing discomfort is a cop-out. Learn to actually look forward to discomfort and realize that it is a barometer indicating that you are extending yourself and that improvement is forthcoming.

(Un)Known

Probably the greatest fear in exploring one's personal performance frontiers is the fear of the unknown. We just don't know how far our minds and bodies can take us in our performance specialties. The newness of these explorations provides little security, few guarantees, and has many risks.

The unknown regions of our performance selves are the reasons for extending ourselves. This is our quest: to see just how far we can go in our particular activities. Yet, many performers are afraid of what they may discover in themselves. The fear of the unknown can be paralyzing. For these performers, this paralysis is often perceived as preferable to what they might discover about themselves.

The fear of the unknown is often the kingpin that organizes the other performance fears. People who have this fear also fear that if they face themselves all their other fears will be opened up and unleashed. So they spend their whole lives avoiding themselves and running from their potentials.

I do not believe in the old adage that "What you don't know won't hurt you." What you don't know—and are afraid to find out—can only hurt you in the long run by limiting your opportunities to grow.

As the fear of failure often masks the fear of success, so the fear of the unknown often masks the fear of the known. It is much easier to plead ignorance than it is to be responsible for knowledge. Maslow (1968) eloquently stated that "a fear of knowing is very deeply a fear of doing, because of the responsibility inherent in new knowledge" (p. 66). It is one thing to learn something, but implicit in this learning is the demand to apply and refine it. This demand for its application and the responsibility of new knowledge can be very threatening. In the light of these fears, many performers prefer to shrink back to the recesses of ignorance and mediocrity.

High-level performers embrace new knowledge as tools for improvement. They use the known as tools for exploring their unknowns. They accept the responsibilities and the demands of the known. They know that their performance levels are always dynamic: Either they are progressing or regressing; there is no status quo.

Ignorance is not bliss. Especially in the presence of options and alternatives, ignorance is copping out and succumbing to self-imposed limitations. Knowledge is power. It is the boat we sail on as we go into our unknown performance frontiers. Sure, the unknown can, at times, be a little scary. Only you can decide whether you are going to run away from it or face it head on.

Overcoming Fears

This chapter may have painted a gloomy picture of how fears can drag down performers. So, what can you do about your fears? It is easy for me to say, "Don't be afraid," or "Relax," but this is of little comfort when you are shaking in your boots before a performance. There are some things you can do to overcome your fears.

Becoming aware of your unique fears is an essential first step in dealing with them. Learn about your fears. Use the major categories of performance fears presented in this chapter as springboards to examine your individual performance fears. You may very well have to peel away different layers of fears in order to find the fear at the core. Remember, if one fear is present, others are probably around.

For example, learn to look at the fears of failure and success together. If you become aware of some fears of failure, ask yourself what possible fears of success you also might have. On the other hand, if you become aware of some fears of success, ask yourself what possible fears of failure you also might have. Each overt fear is usually a mask for a more covert and subtle fear. Learn to peel away the outside layers in order to reach the inner controlling layers of fears.

To become even more aware of your performance fears, answer the following questions:

• Are there patterns or themes of my performance fears?

_____

If yes, what are they? _____

_____

• Am I really prepared for success? _____

What do I fear might happen to me if I become a success?

_____

_____

• What are the absolutely worst things that could happen to me in this performance? (Be very specific.)

_____

_____

_____

• Have any of these "worst things" ever happened before?

_____

If yes, what did I do? _____

_____

• If something similar to one of these "worst things" happens to me in this performance, what could I do?

1. _____

2. _____

3. _____

• If any of these "worsts" happened, what could I do afterwards to prevent them from ever happening again?

_____

_____

- How do I cope with rejection? _____

  _____

  with embarrassment?

  _____

  _____

  with loss, failure, or disappointment?

  _____

  _____

- How can I better mentally prepare or relax so that the chances of these performance fears are reduced?

  _____

  _____

  _____

This last question points to a major strategy in overcoming performance fears. Like most other performance inhibitors, focusing on fear is a self-fulfilling prophecy. For example, if I focus on how afraid I am of being rejected at my next sales presentation, I am actually programming myself to feel rejection. The times to rely on your positive attitudes are when you start to feel the twinges of fear. Trust yourself and believe in your abilities. Remind yourself that everything will turn out all right. In an interview in the *Anglican Digest,* Lichtenberger (1962) beautifully stated, "Fast from fear, and feast on faith" (p. 16). The fearful times are really tests of how much mastery you have over yourself and therefore over your performance specialty.

You will always find fears if you look for them. You can choose to focus on those fears, or you can choose to focus on the specific things in your performance you need to do in order to improve. Fears tend to settle on performers who have stopped progressing and moving ahead. By emphasizing your competencies and by moving forward, you will leave your fears behind.

Next, realize your fears are yours and no one else's. Blaming someone or something else for your fears only serves to strengthen the grasp the fears have on you. Take responsibility for all your actions and attitudes, including your fears. Admit and accept them as *your* fears. At some level of your consciousness, you have allowed your fears to take hold of you. Therefore, if you have allowed them to emerge, believe you also have the power to control them.

A good gimmick you can use in controlling your fears is to laugh at them. That's right, laugh at them. When you feel the same old performance fears creeping up on you, laugh at them, and say such things to yourself as "Here I go again," or "Ha, I'm afraid of my own shadow!" Laughing at yourself gives you a broader perspective. With this perspective you can assert more responsibility over yourself, so laugh at your fears and show them who's the boss!

Keep in mind that no matter how stressful they are, fears are energy. Hence the goal for handling them is not to kill them or get rid of them because, then, you are losing precious energy. On the contrary, the goal for handling your fears is to be in control of yourself. You will then be in a strong position to channel your fears in productive directions or make yourself more immune to them altogether. Specific methods on handling stress and on channeling your performance energies productively will be fully covered in chapter 9.

Remember, some fears do serve valid purposes. Without fear our prehistoric ancestors would have probably been dinner for some beast. The fight or flight response is a well-accepted physiological and psychological principle that describes the human response to potentially dangerous situations. Learn the difference between real fears that may actually be dangerous and those that are illusions. If possible, also learn how to use your fears to mobilize and to accelerate your efforts.

It is okay to excel and succeed. Give yourself permission to do so. Along the way, you will make mistakes, but shrug them off and learn from them. Accept whatever you attain.

Performance results are seldom proportional to our efforts. Sometimes we work really hard for average results. Near the end of his life, Jack Benny, in accepting an award, said, "Well, I really don't deserve this award—but I didn't deserve to be nearsighted either!" Don't worry whether you deserve something or not, why it isn't fair, or how come the results are not proportional to the efforts. Accept whatever comes your way and believe that you deserve it.

Probably the best overall strategy for overcoming your fears is developing yourself as a person as well as a performer. The more sense of self-worth, belief, and trust you develop, the more you will become immune to counterproductive fears. Your performance specialty is a marvelous arena in which to extend yourself. Take this several steps farther and expand this developmental perspective into the rest of your life. Growth, success, risking, change, and knowledge have no room for fears.

Fears are limitations. Learn about them, take responsibility for them, control them, laugh at them, channel them, let them go, and forge ahead. You will then be making great leaps into your performance frontiers.

Chapter 6 Performance Skills

- All of us have experienced fear in our performances. Some fear is valid in that it protects us from injury. But the vast majority of fears are counterproductive and inhibiting. Better understanding and controlling of your performance fears are keys to higher level and more consistent efforts.

- There are five basic categories of performance fears:
    1. The fears of failure and success
    2. The fears of rejection, risk, ridicule, embarrassment, and being discovered as a fraud
    3. The fear of change
    4. The fear of discomfort
    5. The fear of the (un)known

- Fears breed fears. Where there are some fears, there are usually others. One often has to peel through layers of fears to discover the true core fears.

- Based on your understanding of your unique performance fears, the following are some basic strategies you can employ in overcoming those fears:
    1. Realize that fear is energy; therefore, the goal is not to get rid of the fear, but to channel its energy into more productive directions.

2. Instead of worrying about or reacting to the fear, emphasize the tasks or aspects of your performance you need to do well.

3. Take responsibility for your fears and be in control. You might even want to laugh at the absurdity of your fears in order to gain perspective.

4. Personal development is your best fear buster.

- Notes: _____

  _____

  _____

  _____

  _____

  _____

- Additions or changes to your personal performance formula:

  _____

  _____

  _____

  _____

  _____

chapter 7

The Psychology of Doing

Do or not do. There is no trying.
—*The Yoda from* Star Wars: The Empire Strikes Back

*I*n the light of the themes of the previous chapters, it is probably not surprising that high-level performers are characterized as doers. Others may rate these performers as achievers or even superachievers, but when asked how they would evaluate themselves, these performers most often respond with a shrug and say something to the effect of, "I just go out there and do it."

In any effective performance, there is a crucial difference between doing something and trying to do it. This is much more than a semantic distinction; it's often the difference between success and failure. Trying is not doing. Trying is one step before doing. In fact, putting all your efforts into trying is actually setting yourself up for failure.

There are many different variations of trying and all of them are counterproductive. Tryers are often well-intentioned, dedicated, and even noble, but they rarely achieve or maximize much. Tryers will often utter phrases such as "Well, I'll try to do it (but I don't think I can)," "I'll try to have it completed by Monday," or "I'm trying so hard, but I just can't seem to do it."

One of my experiences may help clarify the differences between doing and trying. When I moved out West from the Illinois prairie, I immediately became involved in rock climbing. for those of you who do not know the difference between rock and mountain climbing, rock climbing is that enjoyable activity where we climb up sheer faces of rock with our butts hanging out over 3,000 feet of nothing and say, "My, isn't this relaxing!" Like other formalized activities, rock climbers have their own specialized jargon. They call a "rock" anything from a 3-foot boulder to the 3,000-foot El Capitan in the Yosemite Valley. What they refer to as "scrambling" most of us would need elevators to scale! Rock climbers also have their own specialized system that rates the difficulty of the climb. This system currently ranges from 5.0—essentially climbing up irregular stairs—to 5.13—climbing up a very smooth and vertical (or even overhanging) wall.

My highest rated climb was a 5.7. Now, if I were at the base of a 5.10 rock and had the mentality of a tryer, I would probably say to myself, "I've just gotta make it to the top of this rock." Take a moment, imagine this scene vividly, and repeat this phrase a couple of times to yourself. Say it with great conviction and see what happens to your breathing and to your hands. As I say this phrase, I would grit my teeth, cut short my breathing, have some apprehension in my voice, and probably clench my fists (paradoxically, those parts of me that need to be the most pliable). Tryers frequently set inappropriate and unattainable goals. For them, there are no in-betweens: Either it is total success or abject failure.

When faced with a challenging situation, tryers are very unimaginative problem solvers. To them, there is only one type of adjustment to be made: trying harder. Imagine me climbing this 5.10 rock. After making three or four moves up the rock, I come to a very difficult move. The harder I try to make this difficult move, the more energy I expend, the more frustrated and fearful I become, and the more I lose my climbing rhythm and concentration. Eventually, I become angry, tired, give up, and have to come down.

Tryers are also cruel judges of themselves. In this situation I would probably say to myself, "Boy, I tried so hard to climb that 5.10 rock, but I failed miserably." Tryers are also famous for their generalizing and extrapolating. So I would go on and say, "I'll *never* be able to climb that 5.10 rock. That must mean I will *never be able* to climb any 5.10 rock. I must then be a *terrible* rock climber, and a *worthless* human being.

However, if I had the same abilities, the same experiences, and was at the base of the same rock, but had the mind-set of a doer, I would approach the situation with an entirely different set of attitudes and perspectives. I would probably be saying to myself, "I would like to climb all the way up this rock, but first let's see how well I can climb this first section." Doers set more appropriate and attainable goals. They do not create unnecessary pressures for themselves by setting unrealistic objectives. As a doer at the base of this rock, I would probably be relaxing, conserving my energy, planning my routes, and focusing my concentration on the rock.

Once I started climbing I would be listening for signals from my body so that I could stay in my optimal climbing rhythm. When I came to that same difficult move, I would be much more creative and imaginative in my problem solving. I might take a couple of moves back down to see if there was another route around that tough section. Tryers never even think of that! Even if I could not go any farther, I would come down with a whole different set of perspectives: "Hey, I started climbing (*-ing* term) that 5.10 rock. Maybe next time I can make that difficult move (setting a more appropriate and attainable goal) or find a different route. Then I can climb that upper section. Eventually, I will climb this rock, and I will enjoy myself doing it."

Doers have quite different and more expanded perspectives than tryers. They desire success as much as tryers but approach their performance situations in more realistic ways. Doers also know how to adapt and adjust to changing situations and are creative problem solvers. Doers scale their performance rocks while tryers merely spin their wheels.

Doing Zones

Doers are very aware of their optimal zones of performance. They know that these zones are frequently very narrow and have fine lines on each side of them that are easily crossed. Figure 7.1 illustrates the three Doing Zones.

To reach the Optimal Performance Doing Zone these doers have learned how to intensify, concentrate, and bear down so that they attain their optimal performance rhythms. Especially in very new or very old performance situations, doers have learned that they need to really shift smoothly into their performance gears. What distinguishes their efforts from those of tryers is that doers can shift gears

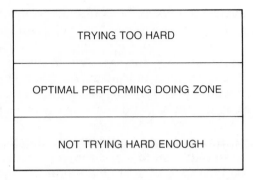

Figure 7.1 Doing zones.

without placing great counterproductive pressures and expectations on themselves. Doers, however, narrow their fields of attention down to the tasks at hand while still allowing their skills and abilities to flow out naturally.

Once in this doing zone, these performers stay conscious of not crossing over the line where they intensify their efforts too much. They know that they have an optimal amount of arousal and that it is very easy to become overly aroused to the point that they are actually working against themselves. Sure, they have to continually put out effort to perform their best, but doers put in much more efficient efforts than tryers.

Remaining in this optimal doing zone requires constant adjustments. Doers stay in their optimal performance zones by exhibiting the same kind of "tight-loose" properties necessary for proper goal setting. They must remain tight with the task by applying themselves, by concentrating well, and by bearing down on the things they need to do. However, they must also remain loose enough to allow their performance rhythms, timings, tempos, and synchronizations to flow out in an integrated manner.

How can you best reach and stay in your optimal doing zone? First, realize that it is a zone that has very fine boundaries on either side of it which, when crossed, lead to the counterproductive efforts of either trying too hard or not trying hard enough. Next, when you are warming up before a rehearsal or performance and your efforts demand a large degree of rhythm and timing, experiment with feeling the extremes of mental and physical rigidity and laxness. Really feel those extremes and then start to find a happy medium between them.

For example, when I am taking my practice golf swings before the first tee, I will take a couple of swings in a very rigid manner, and then I will take a couple of swings in a totally lax manner. I will then take a few swings in seemingly slow motion and then take a few swimgs at a very quick pace. After I have felt the extremes, I will take some swings aimed at eventually finding my comfortable happy medium.

Finally, during the actual performance, when you come to a big point or important sequence and you have the urge to really push harder, use this as a reverse stimulus to ease off and to relax. These temptations to push or to try harder are the quickest ways to take you beyond your optimal performing zone. For example, when I was playing competitive racquetball and I came to a crucial point in the third game, I often felt that I had to really bear down. By charting my games, I learned that when I did bear down I lost 79% of the crucial points. When I learned to recognize my feelings as indications that I was in danger of going beyond my optimal performance zone, I used them as reverse stimuli to ease off, and my charts showed that I won 84% of those crucial points. Especially after midway into a performance, it is important to stay intense enough to remain in your doing zone, but to be aware of the fine line of trying harder.

Staying in this optimal doing zone is much like walking a tightrope: That is, you must have the intensity and concentration to be precise, but you also must have the ease and fluidness to allow your optimal performance rhythms and adjustments to emerge. The greatest danger of falling off your performance tightrope comes from giving in to the temptation of trying harder.

The Myth of Trying Harder

Most of us have been taught that when the performance is going smoothly, that's just fine. But when things are going poorly, what have we been taught to do? Try harder, push harder.

Many of us were raised with the "more is always better" philosophy to problem solving. We were taught that if we tried harder, or put out more effort, we could overcome any obstacle. Persistence and tenacity are very positive qualities, but occasionally we take these to extremes in trying too hard. We then usually end up working against ourselves. As we grew up and developed in our performance specialties, we were unaware that there might have been other approaches to problem solving than just trying harder. McCluggage (1977) capsulized this point well when she said, "Too often, *trying* bespeaks excessive effort, an attempt to overwhelm, and often such trying falls on the other side of *doing*. Less would have hit the mark. Less would have been more" (p. 134). For some of us these remarks seem illogical and even absurd. How can less be more?

It takes many performers a long time to discover that there are fragile performance rhythms and zones that are easily destroyed by trying harder. Golf is a marvelous example of this. There are days when I feel that I have absolutely no rhythm or tempo in my swing. Everything seems foreign and strange. The harder I try to force rhythm and tempo into my swing, the more foreign it becomes. The harder I try to make good contact with the ball, the more I drive it underground! Frustrations breed anger, and anger usually serves to narrow the field of possible solutions to trying even harder. This sequence quickly becomes a vicious circle and usually ends with my contemplating taking up tennis again!

On the other hand, even when I am playing well, there is still a temptation to try harder. After a couple of good strokes or holes, most golfers have experienced a feeling of confidence and approach the next tee saying to themselves, "I'm really going to murder this one!" Well, after the sky clears from all the dismembered turf, we usually see the ball dribbling into the rough. Greed, like frustration, is the kiss of death to any performance rhythm.

Our Western cultures have imbued in us many narrow strategies to problem solving. One of the most prevalent and counterproductive of these is, "If at first you do not succeed, try and try again." There is some validity in this notion. This belief often facilitates perseverance and diligence, but as with most other notions of optimal performance, after a point, this strategy quickly becomes counterproductive. Morehouse and Gross (1977) elaborated by saying, "The perfect idiot who first doesn't succeed because he's doing something wrong tries and tries again. Such practices make the error perfect" (p. 62). Trying and trying harder fosters a tunnel-visioned approach to problem solving that not only blinds the performer to any other possibilities, but also reinforces the error, making it extremely difficult to correct.

Comedienne Lily Tomlin has a wonderful line that goes, "Did you ever wonder why no one ever tries softer?" Think about it. For most of us this statement seems quite illogical. However, it is my contention that *80% of all performance problems occur because the performer is already trying too hard.* Trying harder only serves to push the performer farther off course.

Trying harder sucks us out of our optimal performance zones so that we are working against ourselves. Exercise physiology tells us that muscle contractions are more powerful when they start from a relaxed state. From this base the muscle has a greater range and distance of motion over which to contract; hence, it is more powerful. When we try harder, we never completely allow the muscle to relax, so it is always in some stage of contraction. This not only reduces the range and distance of the contraction, it also fatigues the muscle more quickly. We can use this muscle example as an analogy to performing. That is, we have a greater range of duration of performance energies when we start from a relaxed position.

Another fact from exercise physiology we can apply to our overall performance is that it takes relatively longer for a muscle to relax than it does for it to contract. This relative time difference is amplified when the muscle is fatigued. For example, when I am walking or running, my quadriceps (front thigh) muscles contract as my hamstrings (rear thigh) muscles relax. This complementarity between these two sets of muscles is what propels me. However, when I try harder, I quickly push myself outside of my most efficient stride rhythm so that one set of muscles hasn't fully relaxed before the other set is contracted. Especially when I am fatigued and if I keep on pushing harder, there will come a point where both sets of muscles are contracted at the same time. A pulled hamstring is usually the result.

When I run a 10K race, I usually find that I am running faster in the second half of the race, when I'm supposed to be more fatigued, than in the first half. True, I pace myself, but there always comes a point somewhere between 1 and 2 miles into the race when I say things to myself such as,

"Whew, I'm underway and now I can relax," "Well, I didn't get trampled at the start," "What a beautiful day it is," or "My legs feel really fresh and strong today." Paradoxically, then, when I slow down my mind, my legs speed up in a more powerful and rhythmic fashion. So in the latter parts of the race, I am running faster and actually expending less energy than in the earlier stages. Trying softer keeps me in my optimal performance zone so that I can continually adjust and put out my best efforts.

Sport announcers are fond of commenting, "She's really playing within herself today." What do they mean? This usually indicates that the performer has found her optimal zones and has resisted the temptations of trying harder. From these zones she is then in a better position to listen to signals from her body and to make the appropriate adjustments in form, pace, and tempo so that she can stay in her doing zone.

After you have achieved your optimal performance zone, slow down in order to remain in it. If you have problems achieving it, do not force. Rather, slow down, ease off, shrug your shoulders, and concentrate on the specifics you need to do well. In either case, put your efforts into doing the best you can instead of trying hard to do it.

The bottom line with all of this is *do* whatever you are doing, even if it is at a minimal level of success, effectiveness, or efficiency. Tryers never get on the ladder, and trying harder only takes them farther away from it.

You Cannot Think and Do At the Same Time

Probably the most controversial corollary of the psychology of doing is this: One cannot think and do at the same time. Thinking and doing are two separate processes. Any attempt to combine them usually results in scattered and poor performances. Thinking while doing is really a subtle camouflage for trying.

Think back to your own good performances of the past. Remember those times when your performance was going very well, like you always had imagined it. It might have been presenting to a group, dancing, riding a dirt bike, taking a test, or playing racquetball. At some point during your performance, you might have found yourself saying, "Gee, this is going really well." What happened then? Your performance levels probably dropped dramatically because you were trying to think and do at the same time.

If you doubt the validity of the concept of not being able to think and do at the same time, go play a video game like Pac Man. Try thinking and playing at the same time. Chances are that you will be spending so much time thinking about the possible routes that you will get eaten up! At best, your movements will be very fragmented, lacking the kinds of rhythm and flow you would need to be elusive.

O. J. Simpson was quoted in his biography (Libbey, 1974) as saying, "Thinking is what gets you caught from behind" (p. 180). Trying to think and do at the same time frequently leads to what is called paralysis by analysis. You spend so much time and energy analyzing options and choices that you are unable to execute anything. Thinking while doing short circuits the essential performance pathways of rhythm, tempo, pace, intuition, wisdom, and experience you need for a good effort.

Thinking, talking about, analyzing, reflecting, teaching, or processing use different parts of the brain than pure doing. Not only do these processes divert energies away from performing the activity, but they also foster the misconception that the higher levels of the brain must always control every minute movement of that activity. Korwin (1980) points out that

> There are many things the upper brain cannot do. The upper brain was not developed to control body movements. The upper brain does not "know" what the body does when it moves and does not "know" how to learn new movements. That is all done quite completely by the lower brain. (p. 67)

The brain possesses a marvelous specificity of function. Thinking while doing only serves to cloud this specificity.

For a long time I was bewildered by the case of the football quarterback who called his own plays. He seemed to contradict the principle that one cannot think and do at the same time. I could not understand how a quarterback could remember the dynamics of the previous plays, assess the situation, call the appropriate play, read the defense, and then execute the play well. It wasn't until I had the opportunity to interview a number of quarterbacks at a variety of levels that I found out that the good ones have the ability to continually and completely shift from thinking to doing. In the huddle they are thinking as they call the play. As they break the huddle and walk to the line, they are surveying the defense, but they are also making the transition from thinking to doing. As they start the count, they have shifted to pure doing. (This explains why they sometimes forget the snap count.) Then when the play is in motion, they are in a mode of pure doing. This shifting from thinking to doing and back again is very difficult to master. This difficulty accounts for the trend to have the coaches call the plays so that the quarterback can concentrate more on his own execution.

To be sure, there are times that it is necessary to think, to process, and to analyze. Before and after the performance, as well as during time-outs or breaks in the action, we need to think. But during the action itself, we must do. One of the reasons that many outstanding coaches and teachers were rarely outstanding performers is that their loves of observing, thinking, and analyzing frequently blocked their high-level performing. Once they became a coach or a teacher, they could effectively apply their wisdom in helping others to perform well.

The transition time between thinking and doing may only be a few milliseconds, but it should never overlap. For example, when someone asks me a question, I think about and formulate my answer. Milliseconds later when I answer the question, I am purely doing. The interplay always goes on, but in order to be effective with both processes, thinking and doing must remain separate.

One final example illustrates the need for a separation between thinking and doing. There is a fascinating phenomenon in performance psychology called reminiscence. This phenomenon revolves around the principle that your body remembers much more about an action than does the mind. This is called muscle memory. Think back now to those times when you returned to your activity following a lengthy layoff. Chances are you were pleasantly surprised at how relatively well you performed. This is called reminiscence. Sure you were rusty, but you probably experienced an ease of movement that was encouraging. You probably concentrated differently because the once well-known performance environment was now a little strange to you. Most of all, you had fun.

What happened the next time out? Probably you tried a little harder, analyzed and dissected your skills more, became more competitive, and expected more. Your efforts then became increasingly fragmented. The results were probably poorer and you enjoyed yourself less.

What caused the differences between these two outings? The first time those specific and well-learned motor skills were remembered (or reminisced) by your body. Because your mind was occupied with the strangeness of the situation, these skills could naturally flow out in an integrated manner. As soon as you became more familiar with the surroundings, you probably started directing your mind to thinking, trying harder, isolating and separating, analyzing, and expecting more. This shift served to put up roadblocks to the performance pathways of your skills and reminiscences. In short, you became too comfortable and smart for your own good and started to force things.

It should not be surprising to you that the cornerstone of doing (as well as resisting the temptations of trying harder or trying to think and do at the same time) revolves around our old friend trust. If you have learned and practiced properly, your body knows what to do, so let it. Thinking, processing, and analyzing while doing are all subtle forms of distrust.

With respect to Mr. Spock of *Star Trek* fame, there comes a time in performing when logic is inappropriate and counterproductive. Korwin (1980) concluded that "natural body movements are based on faith not logic" (p. 69). McCluggage (1977) went as far as to say that "logic owns a monkey-wrench factory" (p. 114). The more I analyze how or why I am doing something during a performance, the less I will be able to do anything about it.

It has been said that the best performers are the ones who are frequently unaware of what they are doing. They are purely doing. Quite often, we have to spend as much time and energy in unlearning, turning off, and letting go as we spend in learning, tuning into, and focusing. The trick is knowing when to do each.

These concepts are not new. They have been said in many different ways throughout history, but perhaps no more profoundly and beautifully than by the Chinese philosopher Lao Tse who posed, "The way to do is to be." It is as simple—and challenging—as that.

Doing is Proving

There is an old saying that goes, "Talk is cheap." I would like to add, ". . . but doing is proving." Besides spending much time trying to reach inappropriate goals and thinking instead of acting, tryers love to analyze, speculate, and talk about their performance specialties. Doers, on the other hand, know when it is helpful to analyze and to speculate, but also know that they will obtain their best information on their performance specialties from the experience of doing it.

Tryers put a great deal of unfair pressure on themselves in trying to excel. One good example of this is the way many tryers train. They believe that if a little of a particular training approach is good, more must always be better. These people seldom listen to their bodies and rarely allow themselves to recuperate. As a result, tryers become very susceptible to injuries and stagnation. Training hard at all costs until their training becomes a compulsion, they are the classic overtrainers. When their performances invariably suffer, their only response to this is to try and train even harder.

As much as they talk about pressure and stress, a great deal of it is self-imposed. Very often, the root of this pressure and compulsion is due to their expectations to be perfect.

Perfectionism

Whenever I work with a performer who says, "Well, I'm a perfectionist," I mentally hit myself in the head and say to myself, "Oh, this is going to take a long time!" Perfectionism is the pinnacle of the tryer's mentality. They are the prototypical musturbaters. To these performers, perfectionism means the absence of any faults. However, in reality their quests for perfectionism are self-defeating in that the harder they try to be perfect (without any faults), the more aware they become of their imperfections. These imperfections are really their unique qualities that make them individuals, but they look on these uniquenesses as deficiencies. The more they reject these parts of themselves, the more they discover that they are slipping away from their perfect ideals. You can probably guess how they react to this. They try even harder to be perfect. Their search for the golden fleece of perfectionism, in the long run, only promotes regression and poor performances.

Contrary to popular opinion, perfectionists are not the achievers we (or they) think they are. Perfectionists spend an inordinate amount of time and energy spinning their wheels, going off on counterproductive tangents, and trying harder and harder. They live with constant doubts, frustrations, and fears. For them every performing event becomes a potential threat to their ideals of perfection. These people frequently set inappropriate and unattainable goals to suit what they believe to be their conceptions of perfection; hence, they usually set themselves up for failure and disappointment. They fear such failures, but their demands for perfection will not allow them to set more realistic goals; therefore, perfectionists often become swallowed up in the maelstrom of fear, failure, and expectations.

The bulimarexic is an excellent example of the perfectionist. Bulimarexia (The Gorge-Purge Syndrome, or Bulimia) is an eating disorder that is sadly increasing among our young women performers as well as in other segments of the population. These women are so obsessed with their weight and body image that they go on radical "diets" to achieve the perfect image. Whether they are a dancer, gymnast, swimmer, or runner, they believe that dieting will not only transform them into the perfect body, but will also be measures of their self-control, commitment, dedication, and willpower. One can guess what usually happens. Because willpower is a finite energy, there will come a time when they succumb, go to the other extreme, and binge eat. In order to relieve the massive amounts of food (as well as the accompanying feelings of guilt and self-hate), they vomit or use laxatives and diuretics. Then they return to their diets with more resolve and willpower, believing that "if only I were a better person, then I could stick to this diet." But the results are always the same. This cycle soon becomes out of control and all too automatic. What started out as a quest for perfectionism evolved into tragedy.

Perfect is really an interesting word. Its suffix (*-fect*) means "to fall" as in *infect* ("fall into") and *defect* ("fall out of"). *Perfect* literally means "to fall through." The ancient Romans looked at perfectionism not as the absence of faults, the way we have bastardized the concept today, but as falling through life. To them, perfectionism was living life, experiencing life, falling on your face occasionally, but always getting up, learning from the experience and continuing. They looked forward to new experiences, learned from them, and integrated these learnings into their lives. The hallmarks of their conceptions of perfectionism were not trying hard to reach some unattainable ideal, but experiencing, accepting, and trusting themselves.

Today, we have skewed these classic notions of perfectionism so that they now go hand in hand with the self-defeating processes of trying harder, setting unrealistic expectations, and mistrusting self. Perfectionists may be seen as dedicated or even noble, but their tryer's mentality dooms them to frustration and mediocrity.

Doers aspire to accomplish just as much as tryers, but their pursuits are grounded in acceptance, belief, and awareness of self. Doers have standards, goals, and needs, but they are based on reality instead of on some unattainable ideal of what they should be. In short, tryers try, but doers do.

The Process of Doing

I am always amused by the question, "Okay, so how do I try to start doing?" Die-hard tryers will wait around expecting some magic wand to pass over them and magically turn them into doers! Just start doing. Get on your performance ladder and begin climbing, and as you do, then and only then, will you be able to modify your mind-set away from that of a tryer to one of a doer.

Doers accept all aspects of themselves—the good as well as the bad. They know that in order to maximize any of their good qualities or transform any of their counterproductive qualities, they first must embrace these qualities as parts of themselves.

Tryers spend much time talking, which frequently takes the forms of blaming, placating, complaining, making excuses, and worrying. The gist of their conversation is, "If only": "If only I had more time to prepare," "If only the wind had not blown," and "If only I had better teachers and equipment." Tryers spend most of their time either reliving memories and nightmares in the past, or fantasizing about perfection in the future. They are often quite unaware of what is occurring at the moment.

Doers spend most of their time in the present. Viewing events on a situation-by-situation basis, they appreciate the newness and uniqueness that each performance situation presents. Although they may spend some time analyzing a problem, they rarely worry about it. As the embodiments of the old Roman conceptions of perfection, they are more apt to assume full responsibility for their actions and learn from them. In the process, they continually strive for improvement and have fun doing it.

There are numerous aspects to doing and trying. In Table 7.1, each mind-set is summarized so that the differences between doing and trying can be more clearly delineated.

So, start doing and continue doing. In the end, doing begets doing. It promotes momentum, self-acceptance, purpose, learning from experience, direction, and the trust to do again. Doing is proving to yourself that you cannot only attain your goals, but become the kind of performer you have always strived to be.

Table 7.1   Comparison of the Doing and Trying Mind-Sets

Doing	Trying
Optimistic; focuses on actualizing and achieving; makes conscious choices to build up	Pessimistic: focuses on deficiencies and limitations; continually tears self down and makes little effort to affirm
Listens to signals from self; seeks optimal performance zones	Pushes too hard; believes that more is always better
Trusts self; simply goes about doing the task	Thinks, analyzes, and talks about the task instead of doing it
Honestly evaluates self and performances; takes responsibility for mistakes and failures; learns from them	Judges self and others; blames and makes excuses for mistakes and failures; frequently repeats them
Sets appropriate and attainable goals	Sets ill-defined, inappropriate, and unattainable goals

Table 7.1 cont.

Table 7.1 cont. Comparison of the Doing and Trying Mind-Sets

Doing	Trying
Spends time in the present	Spends time in the past or future; expectations based in past or future
Continually ponders, incubates, and revises plans; flexible	Worries; feels bound by outdated plans; rigid
Perceives always in process of succeeding or achieving	Perceives only in the extremes of total success or failure; no in-betweens
Creative problem solver; employs a variety of problem-solving strategies	Unimaginative problem solver; solely employs the "try harder" strategy
Sets priorities and gives commitments	Inconsistent and low levels of seting priorities and commitments, rarely following through on them
Continually learns, integrates, and synthesizes	Isolated and segmented learning; little continuity between learnings
Accepts and looks forward to change as opportunities for growth and improvement	Resists and fears change; focuses on what may be lost from any potential change; procrastinates
Maintains balance in life	Some areas in life are out of balance with others; probably overtrains
Maintains perspective; genuinely enjoys the activity; has a sense of humor	Tunnel-visioned; little perspective; too serious
Accepts and likes self	Perfectionist; generalizes and extrapolates judgments; has difficulty accepting self at times

Chapter 7 Performance Skills

- A profound psychological difference exists between doing something and trying to do something. Doers set more realistic goals, make more appropriate adjustments, and build upon their positive qualities. Tryers most often spin their wheels and go off on counter-productive tangents.

- Although bearing down is beneficial in reaching one's doing zone, there is a very fine line that, once crossed, pushes the performer beyond optimal functioning. More is not always better. Often, when things are not going well, it is due to trying too hard already. In those situations learn to try softer, slow down, relax, or ease off, and you will be pleasantly surprised at how your efforts improve.

- You cannot think and do at the same time. Thinking while doing is really a subtle form of trying. There is a time for thinking, but it is not during the actual effort. Think ahead and reflect afterwards, but during the action, stay in a mode of pure doing.

- Doers accept themselves whereas tryers tend to be perfectionists. Do whatever you are doing and build upon that. Let the tryers try to do; you just do what you need to do.

- Notes: _____

  _____

  _____

  _____

  _____

- Additions or changes to your personal performance formula:

  _____

  _____

  _____

  _____

chapter 8

Igniting Your Performances

So I must become purposeless—on purpose?
—Eugen Herrigel in Zen in the Art of Archery

Concentration is the name of the game. It is the heart of any personal performance formula. If you want to apply your skills and experiences, tap into your potentials, expand your performance frontiers, and become a success, you have to concentrate. But just what does concentration mean?

If you asked 20 performers—even from the same discipline—to list all those factors essential to their concentration, you would receive 20 divergent lists. Of course, some similarities would occur among the lists, but each performer would have unique emphases and keys to concentration, separating his or her list from everyone else's.

The Scope of Concentration

Much of the confusion and ignorance about the word *concentration* stems from the fact that it has been referred to on such general levels for so long that it now is frequently used as a catchall word for anything remotely related to the mental aspects of an activity. The term can mean just about anything when used in phrases such as "I lost my concentration," "My concentration slipped," "All I have to do is concentrate," and "If only I could concentrate better." When used in such vague ways it is no wonder that performers do not know how to apply it more efficiently.

Concentration is a very complicated concept, employing many parts of the brain—frequently, at the same time.

Concentration can be highly tuned for a short duration activity such as sprinting, answering a question, and weight lifting, or it can be extended for a long duration activity such as participating in a triathlon, presenting a business-training seminar, and playing poker for 12 hours. In any case, concentration must be directed, flexible, and multipurposed enough to adapt to a variety of demands and situations.

As a working definition, I would like to use Hill's (1979) conception of concentration. He stated that "concentration is the act of focusing the mind on a given desire until the ways and means for its realization have been worked out and successfully put into operation" (p. 5). This definition raises several points: First, concentration is dependent on the understanding of one's own desires, needs, and subsequent goals and objectives; second, concentration is a creative process that finds solutions to obstacles and problems; and finally, concentration is strengthened as it is applied in an activity.

Tony Jacklin, the British golfer, referred to the mental aspects of his game as his "cocoon of concentration." During these times he would block out all external distractions and zero in on his game. He said that once he was in his cocoon he could sense almost inperceptible changes in the wind, terrain, and the lie of the ball so that he could make the appropriate adjustments to his aim and swing. Without his cocoon he believed that he could never sense such changes, much less execute the shots.

Concentration, then, is a narrowing and structuring of the scope of emphasis. As in looking through a telescope, the only defined region is that which is in the field in view. All the rest of the universe at that time is irrelevant. Concentration defines what is to be viewed in performance efforts.

Con-cen-tration

Within recent years, concentration has been increasingly referred to as a unification of mind and body. Even in nonphysical activities, this view of concentration seeks to bring together all the individual's performance energies. Charlotte Selver (cited in McCluggage, 1977) best refers to this conception as *con-cen-tration*. She literally saw concentration as "a coming to a mutual center" (p. 132). Figure 8.1 represents this conception of concentration. Viewed in this way, concentrating brings together the mind and the body, and all one's skills and abilities, prior experiences, intuitions, roles, and emphases to a unified center from which they can be directed and applied.

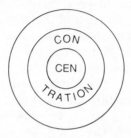

Figure 8.1 Concentration—coming to a mutual center.

Effective concentration is more of a blending than a trying, more of a natural outpouring than an artificial forcing, and more of a dynamic process than a static state. It is based in a unifying center that organizes and combines all performance qualities. From this center these energies can then be channeled with a specific focus.

Concentration is not really magical or mystical. To better understand it, let's break it down into its three major components. Parts of these components overlap, but each has its own unique emphases and dynamics.

Intensity

Historically, concentration was notoriously equated with trying harder. Today, this erroneous notion is usually subsumed under the heading of *intensity,* which is the most overused and misunderstood performance concept in existence. Coaches, managers, leaders, teachers, and performers love using the word. They believe that this word will be the panacea for all their performance problems. However, used in this way, intensity only serves to push people out of their optimal performance zones.

The key of effectively using intensity is not to try harder, but to work smarter. This implies utilizing existing energies in more focused ways. True intensity means finding energy and strength *in* you (literally, *in-tension*) instead of trying to find external sources.

The analogy of a magnifying glass in the sun conveys the correct use of intensity. When we were kids, many of us used to set fire to a piece of paper with only the aid of a magnifying glass. We discovered that the magnifying glass intensified the existing rays of the sun in a more concentrated manner. High achievers have learned to use the idea of intensity as their performance magnifying glasses to concentrate, to focus, and to direct their abilities and energies so that it ignites their performances. On the other hand, those who employ the trying-harder approach to intensity have no magnifying glasses but try to find seven more suns to start the fire!

Thus, the effective uses of intensity are combined, and then the existing skills, drives, and experiences are directed in efficient ways. As this concentration of performance qualities is assembled, it must then be directed. This process is most often referred to as focusing.

Focusing

Concentration and intensity are increasingly being combined and referred to as *focusing*. You might have already become aware that whenever I emphasize an important point, I use the word *focus*. This concept connotes marvelous images of those specifics you need to do.

In most ball sports, the first thing we were told was to watch the ball. What our teachers were really saying was to focus on the ball. Just as the physiological process of focusing "locks in" all of our energies on the object, the psychological process of focusing locks in all our concentration on the task at hand. Morehouse and Gross (1977) stated,

> Focusing is the essence of concentration in which you are using your senses to make small adjustments in timing and rhythm to match the work and eliminate extraneous movement and mental acitivity. . . . You can think too much but you can never focus too sharply. (p.38)

Granted, there is some danger in becoming so rigidly locked in that you develop tunnel vision and cannot make the necessary adjustments; however, sharply focusing on execution is the essential component in controlling your performance.

Focusing is the narrowing element of concentration. It is that function that pinpoints the objective of efforts. As rigid as this function appears, it must also be adaptable. Just as the eye has to continually refocus on different objects and adjust as conditions change, so must performers learn how to refocus their concentration to different objectives and adjust as conditions change. Hence, effective concentration is a dynamic process that involves continuously tuning into different objectives. In this sense, concentration must also be viewed in a larger context of attention and awareness.

Attention and Awareness

Although concentration may imply one single-focused state, it is far from static. The difficult aspect about concentration is that it has to function on several levels simultaneously. Effective and enduring concentration involves an interplay between the mental concepts of attention and of awareness. Attention involves a specifying and pinpointing of perspective. Attention is more of an active process that expands energy (e.g., paying attention); awareness is more of a receptive process that takes in the bigger picture (e.g., becoming aware).

Both attention and awareness must be used in conjunction with one another in order to attain high and balanced levels of concentration. For example, a soccer or hockey goalie must be aware of the play developing against him and of where all the players are at any given moment, but he must also pay specific attention to the ball or puch as it is shot at him. During sales presentations, good salespeople must pay strict attention to what they are saying and how they are saying it, but they also must be aware of how the prospect is receiving their messages, where they are in the sales process, and what else is needed. A singer must remember the specific lyrics, but also must be aware of and blend in with the accompaniment. A good basketball player must have good peripheral vision (awareness) in searching for possible passes, but when he is shooting, he must focus only on the basket (attention). Even a forklift operator must pay attention to a particular pallet as he stacks it, but also must be aware of the whole stack. So, attention and awareness are indispensible complements to overall effective concentration.

The interplay between attention and awareness is what Gestalt psychologists and therapists call the figure and the ground, respectively. To clarify this, look out of your window and focus on any object outside. This object is the figure to which you are paying attention. The area defined by the window frame is the ground of which you are aware. Broad and effective concentration depends on the ability to shift to and from the figure and the ground. McCluggage (1977) stated the distinction in this way:

> Concentration is a flexible awareness of what is important and what is not important to the task-of-the-moment. It is a clear differentiating between which is the **figure** and which is the **ground**. It is attending to the figure while being aware of the ground. (P. 127)

During any activity, performers really operate on two mental wavelengths simultaneously: a broad and general one that gets them "in the ballpark" of concentration (i.e., awareness) and a more specific and narrow one that focuses them on the subject at hand (i.e., attention).

In many performances the situation can rapidly change. This implies that the figure of one's concentration must also change (e.g., shifting attention from one ski gate to another or shifting from selling to servicing). As the emphases change during an event, performers must continually attend to making the necessary adjustments so that they stay "in tune." Using the analogy of a microscope, effective viewing (performing) is an ongoing process of employing both the coarse adjustment knob (awareness) to obtain the field and the fine adjustment knob (attention) to focus in on the subject.

The simultaneous use of attention and awareness is what enables a performer to anticipate, adapt, endure, create, respond more quickly, conserve energy, put in more consistent efforts, and increase the overall levels of effectiveness. The interplay between paying attention and becoming aware is the window in your cocoon of concentration.

Strengthening and refining these complementary processes will improve both the depth and breadth of your concentrating and, thus, your performances. Let's take a closer look at how this can be accomplished.

Improving Concentration

It is hoped that you now have a better understanding of the major components to effective concentration. As with any other peformance emphasis, improvement must start with where you are now, so answer the following questions:

- What things do you focus on when you are concentrating well?

  _____

  _____

- What are the patterns of your lapses of concentration?

  _____

  _____

- How does trying harder affect your concentration?

  _____

  _____

    fear? _____

  _____

    anger? _____

  _____

- When and how are you most apt to become distracted?

  _____

  _____

  _____

- What specific things do you need to focus on to improve your concentration?

  _____

  _____

  _____

There are definite patterns to all of our effective as well as ineffective concentration experiences. We become distracted by the same types of events and bear down well under a different sort of circumstances. Continually ask yourself about the general patterns of your concentration using the questions listed previously or using other more specific questions.

Focusing In

Improving your overall abilities of concentration is dependent on your being able to focus and apply yourself to one thing at a time. To improve, begin by focusing on one tiny aspect of your performance specialty during your next rehearsal or practice. See how long you can concentrate solely on it. The longer you focus on it, the more you will encounter lapses in concentration and distractions, and the more your mind will wander. That's okay, so don't worry right now. Just focus on your task at hand.

For example, during a volleyball practice I want to focus just on how I set the ball. I want to get to the point where my whole reality revolves around my setting of the ball. I want to see just how far and for how long I can concentrate on this. Everything else—serving, spiking, digging out balls, and blocking—must, for the time being, take a back seat to my focusing on setting the ball. Or if I am concentrating on the accuracy of my typing, I would focus just on that. Speed will play a secondary role to accuracy. I want to be acutely aware of typing everything correctly. If I become distracted or my mind wanders, I will simply return to my priority at hand—typing accurately. Notice that my emphasis is on accuracy, not on not making mistakes. This is an important distinction we will further explore in chapter 11.

You may want to expand on this exercise by focusing on one thing in the rest of your life as well: a flower, a child playing, a cloud, your breathing, your posture, or anything else that comes into your mind. If you are able to concentrate well in the other areas of your life, you will be able to concentrate more effectively in your performance specialty. Therefore, apply yourself. You will not be conspicuous when you are doing these exercises, so don't worry about embarrassing yourself when you are practicing your focusing. You will soon discover that there is even a kind of satisfaction in being able to apply yourself in this manner.

Sustaining Concentration

After you have learned to focus more deeply, the next step is learning to sustain it. The key to consistent performances is sustained concentration. As in building up physical endurance, effective concentration implies building up mental endurance. To do this, start out by expanding the time you focus on a thing. With each day, focus on something for a little longer. This is where the issues of the optimal doing zone and pacing yourself come into play again. The best way to remain in your range is to learn how to ease off once you have reached your optimal doing zone. Trying harder will only push you out of this zone and decrease your mental endurance.

A very effective exercise to help all types of performers increase the endurance of their concentration is having them go for long rides alone in the country for the amount of time their upcoming performances are expected to last. If, for example, their performances are expected to last 2 hours, have them go for at least a 2-hour ride to experience how it feels to concentrate for that duration of time. Too often, performers only plan the first part of their efforts and do not develop the sense of the overall duration of the effort. This leads to lapses of concentration, usually in the second half of the performance. Going out for such rides will give them opportunities to develop this sense and will reinforce that they are in control of their concentration.

For athletes and other physical performers, I recommend a bicycle ride in the country. If they are not familiar with bicycling, all the better, for it forces them to adapt to a foreign situation. This ride provides just enough discomfort to make them continuously adapt both physically and mentally. For nonphysical performing artists and business people, a car ride (with the radio off) in the country serves a similar purpose. Sitting for such a long time adds the dimension of physical fatigue to inactivity. With this fatigue they then have the opportunity to learn how to cope with the mental discomfort. Learning how to cope with the discomforts over a duration of time is a cornerstone in developing sustained concentration.

An issue that frequently arises is learning how to pace, relax, and take little mental time-outs during a prolonged activity. Pacing is essential. If people are going to be concentrating for 3 hours, they have to establish this time frame in their plans. Relaxing before and during the effort is also crucial to maintaining concentration. Especially during long efforts, all performers must know just how long they can sustain their intensity before they need a break. These little relaxation breaks may range from shrugging their shoulders to gazing at the scenery to calling a time-out to take in refreshments. All of us have a limit to the length of time we can attend to any one activity. Taking short breaks enables us to lengthen our concentration span and helps us to join together more attention segments.

As you learn how to improve the depth and duration of your concentration, distractions will actually become less of an issue. Distractions, lapses in concentration, fading intensity, going off on tangents, blanking out, the mind wandering, and just plain giving up are due to not focusing well on the tasks at hand. When the mind is not disciplined, you will be susceptible to these counterproductive directions.

Remember, focusing on the thing you need to do well is the best insurance against distractions. Even if you do become distracted, your mental discipline and goals will bring you back on track more quickly. Concentrating well and sustaining your concentration for long periods of time are skills. So it makes sense that the more you practice them in a variety of situations, the more they will become a positive habit. Once these skills become a habit, you will become much more immune to distractions, for you will have realized that it is much more satisfying to be able to concentrate well than it is to go off on tangents.

The Interplay Between Attention and Awareness

Attention and awareness, as well as their interplay, must be developed and refined in order to achieve consistent and effective yet flexible and adaptive levels of concentration. As you develop these skills, you will be increasingly able to control, pace, and sustain all your efforts.

In order to become more aware of your forms of attention and awareness, you will need a quiet place to do the following exercise:

1. Take the phone off the hook, lower or turn off the lights, light a candle, find a comfortable position, and relax.

2. Once you are relaxed, spend a good minute or so focusing on the flame of the candle. Feel how all your mental energies zero in only on that flame.

3. While you are still looking at the flame, become aware of all the objects in the room in your field of vision. See how the flame lights the objects. Take it all in; see the whole.

4. Now, zero back in on the flame.

5. And then expand your awareness back to the surrounding area.

Continue this interplay for four or five more exchanges. Notice the differences in how you feel when you shift from a focused single object to an all-encompassing scene. Develop a sense for what feelings, sensations, and mental dynamics are involved in paying attention versus being aware.

You may wish to further explore this interplay using a large painting or photograph, or even by looking out the window. In each case the frame defines your region of concentration or awareness. Pick out one object in your field and zero in on it. As you continue to look at it, expand your awareness back to the whole region. As you become more aware, another individual part of this field may emerge. Shift your attention to it, focus on it, and then become aware again of the whole.

Throughout this interplay, continue to feel the mental differences between attending one point versus being aware of the whole picture. Continue this interplay for a couple of more exchanges, each time zeroing in on a new object that has emerged from your awareness. End this exercise by becoming keenly aware of the whole field.

Practice the dynamics of this interplay for about a week; then extend this exercise to your practice or rehearsal sessions of your activity. Pay particular attention to one single emphasis and then let it merge back into the whole. Become more aware of the whole of your efforts and let a new emphasis emerge to which you will then pay attention. For example, while running I might first pay attention to how my feet strike the ground; then I will become aware of just myself running. Later I might pay attention to how I am holding my arms and again merge back into my overall awareness. Next, I might pay attention to how I toe off, but I always end with being aware of my whole self running.

As you practice these skills, you will become more effective in achieving deeper levels of attention and awareness as well as become more efficient in shifting between them. You will soon discover that this process is like flexing a muscle. Each time you contract the muscle (pay attention), the more focused and forceful the contraction becomes. Each time you relax the muscle (become aware), the more you discover how it relates to other muscles and to you as a whole.

Developing each function is important, but developing the interplay between attention and awareness is crucial for sustained and adaptive performances. With these you have more mental gears in which to shift during a performance. As you improve on these elements of concentration, you will discover how truly intense, expansive, and sustained your overall concentration can be.

Conclusion

You can now see that effective concentration depends on many interrelated processes. Some of these processes may initially seem to be inconsistent or contradictory with each other, but as you improve, you will see how they fit in with one another. At one level, focusing is a rigid locking in of one's mental energy to the tasks at hand. Yet, at deeper levels, there also exists a flexible and dynamic interplay between attention and awareness—between figure and ground—that continuously tunes the mental energies into the most effective and adaptable wavelengths.

Understanding and refining these mental processes and interactions are really great challenges in themselves. As they become more refined, an inherent joy evolves in the ability to concentrate for its own sake. You will then be able to more effectively control and channel a greater proportion of all your energies to your performances. Concentration is control, and control is the conductor to better performances.

Chapter 8 Performance Skills

- Concentration is the heart of any personal performance formula; it is a skill and, as such, can be improved.

- Effective concentrating exhibits the same tight-loose properties of effective goal setting. When performers are concentrating well, they are not only locked into their tasks at hand, but are also opened up to the proper adjustments that need to be made.

- Proper concentration is increasingly referred to in terms of "a coming together to a mutual center." Effective concentration combines existing skills and energies as well as directs them in a purposeful manner.

- The three major independent elements to concentration are (a) intensity, (b) focusing, and (c) attention and awareness. These elements may overlap a bit, but each has its unique emphases that must be developed.

- There are things you can do to increase the depth, breadth, duration, resistance to distractions, and dynamics of your concentrating. Just as in practicing a physical skill, by working on your mental abilities, you can improve your concentration and, hence, subsequent performances.

- Notes: _____

  _____

  _____

  _____

  _____

  _____

- Additions or changes to your personal performance formula:

  _____

  _____

  _____

  _____

  _____

chapter 9

Surfing on Your Energy Wave

That which will kindle lightning must first for a long time be a cloud.
—Nietzche

"**I**f I only had more energy." "Let me have a candy bar and I'll get more energy." "More energy, people!" "The team must be low on energy today." Just what does all of this mean?

Like attitude and concentration, energy is one of those vague and over-generalized performance terms that involves many misconceptions. We use words like *stress, pressure, psych, arousal, tension, freezing, blanking,* and even *karma* to refer to different forms of energy. Some performers go as far as attaching almost magical connotations to energy. Believing that external concoctions will enhance their performance energies, they rely on devices such as anabolic steroids, diet fads, megavitamins, fancy equipment, ointments, pep talks, and various rituals to help them perform better.

Many performers of all kinds are satisfied to refer to energy on such general levels. They don't know much about their energies in relationship to performing and are usually unwilling to explore this relationship any further. They hope that all their energies will somehow come together for the performances. However, more times than not, what usually happens is that they give flat, fragmented, and mediocre efforts.

The purpose of this chapter is to present an overview of the concept of energy. Along with learning about the different forms of performance energy, you will also learn how to control and channel energy, how to relax, and how to more effectively apply energy in pressure situations.

The Reservoir of Energy

Energy is life. As it relates to performing, energy is all those existing internal physical and mental resources that can be directed to the efforts at hand. Physical energy is most often referred to as strength, endurance, speed, power, skill, agility, and grace. Mental energy is most often referred to as motivation, confidence, concentration, drive, and poise. Performance energies are the products of our training and rehearsing, mental preparation, goals and priorities, rest and recuperation, nutrition, desire, dedication, and concentration. The better we physically and mentally prepare, the greater our reservoir of performance energies and sense of control over channeling these energies into effective efforts.

Locus of Control

A critical point to understand about all forms of energy is that they are neither good nor bad; they are neutral. Rather, it is our unique reactions to pressurized situations that determine whether our performance energies will be productive or counterproductive. That is why, given the same circumstances, some performers fold while others flourish. Remember when the Cincinnati Reds were a dynasty in the 1970s? In the seventh game of the 1975 World Series, The score was tied with two outs in the bottom of the ninth inning, and Pete Rose made it around to third base. Under tremendous pressure, and while the other team was having a conference at the mound, Rose turned to his third base coach and said, "Boy, this is fun!" Given the same circumstances, most of us would be shaking in our boots. This ability to channel pressure into higher performance levels is one of the things that has made Pete Rose one of the greatest players in the history of baseball.

This self-determination of the direction of energy is called locus of control. It is based on the precept that although you may not have total control over a performance situation, you do have control over your reactions and interactions within that situation. This issue is based on the classic distinction that no one makes me angry, happy, fearful, envious, joyful, or frustrated. I make myself that way or I allow someone else to do it to me. In either case, at some level of my consciousness, I am making the decisions governing my responses.

When you look at it, we have little control over any of the situations in our lives, but we do have a wide scope of options in dealing with those situations. I do not have control over my boss giving me an assignment, but I do have control of when and how I accomplish it. I do not have complete control over the outcome of a game, but I do have control of how I play my position in that game. I do not have control over a flash bulb going off in my face, but I do have control of how I react to that distraction and how quickly I get back on course.

Once you have a better understanding of what you can and cannot control, and for what you are and are not responsible, you will be better able to conserve and channel your performance energies. The captain of your performance ship is you—not your supervisors, coaches, or teachers. They can only give input and advice. *You* must make the decisions and produce the efforts. Although you cannot completely control the seas of the performance situations, you can control the navigating of your ship toward the port of success.

Energy Assessment

In order to become aware of your reservoir of energy, you must determine the patterns that add or detract from your energy stores. List below all those factors (no matter how remote) that detract from or sap your performance energies. Take your time and compile as complete a list as possible.

_____	_____	_____
_____	_____	_____
_____	_____	_____
_____	_____	_____

Some factors might be anxiety, sleep problems, poor nutrition, overtraining, negative attitudes, illness or injuries, conflicts with teammates or coaches, fear, and troubles at home or with personal relationships. Not being able to keep your mind on the tasks at hand usually signals that there are energy leaks somewhere in your life.

Now list all those factors that promote or add to your performance energies. Again, take your time and be specific.

_____	_____	
_____	_____	_____
_____	_____	_____
_____	_____	_____

Some of these factors might include previous successes, optimistic attitudes, good support systems, good health and fitness levels, proper nutrition, genuine enjoyment in your activity, proper recuperation and pacing, focused concentration, clearly defined goals, positive practice environments, balanced lifestyle, and belief in self.

Compare these two lists to find relationships between the factors. You might discover that some of these factors are on the opposite sides of the same issue. For example, anxiety in poor performances and eagerness in good performances are opposite sides of the same issue. Other relationships might be between lethargy and relaxation, between overtraining and optimal training, between fuzzy and focused concentration, between conflict and cooperation, or between competitiveness and creativity. Often, when a necessary factor is ill-defined or missing altogether, a related but counterproductive factor will take its place.

These lists are a good start. You might want to return to them, and break down these counterproductive and productive factors even further. For example, poor nutrition may be broken down into too much junk food, not eating breakfast, or too much red meat. On the other list, good support systems may be broken down into good coaching, open and honest communication, consistent encouragement from family and friends, cooperative teammates, and your support of others.

Remember, the villain of performance energies is generality. Hence, the key to understanding your performance energies better is to continually define and redefine your own unique factors as specifically as possible. By doing so, you will take much of the mystery out of performance energies and will put yourself in a better position to control them effectively.

Arousal and Stress

Of the many categories of energy, the two on which most of the others hinge are arousal and stress. Each has its mental and physiological components. Let's take a closer look at each.

Arousal

All of us can remember times of being so frightened that we became keenly aware of everything. Our senses running in high gear and our minds going a mile a minute, we anticipated everything and were prepared to react to anything. In short, we were energized. We have also heard of instances where a mother lifted a car off her pinned child, a man ran like the wind to escape a mugger, or a woman discarded her crutches to save her cat from a burning house. The question is, How do we attain such energy levels?

Although these are extreme examples, we all become energized like this to varying degrees in our everyday lives. *Arousal* is the term that most often represents those states where our bodies become energized and our minds become superfocused. We need arousal to cross a street or to throw a football. The key is learning how to channel our arousal levels in the most appropriate directions.

A classic energy maxim called the Yerkes-Dodson Law states that no matter the skill, increasing the levels of arousal is beneficial to performances, but just to a point. At some point there is a fine line where any additional arousal will become counterproductive and the performance will suffer. The relationship between arousal and performance resembles an inverted—U. In Figure 9.1 an example of the typical arousal curve is provided. Arousal organizes, intensifies, and directs our mental and physiological performance

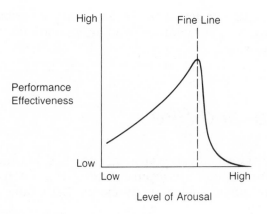

Figure 9.1 A typical arousal curve.

energies—but just to a point. Like walking on a ridge, our view becomes more expanded as we climb to the crest, but if we take any additional steps, we start going downhill and our view narrows.

Oxendine (1970) used this notion of the arousal curve to develop arousal curves for different motor skills. He showed that the more gross or power oriented the motor skills, the higher the level of arousal that is needed to execute them properly. For example, football blocking requires higher levels of arousal than ballet, swimming requires more than putting, and power lifting requires more than shooting free throws. However, no matter the motor skills, each of these activities has a similar arousal curve that includes the same fine line where any additional arousal becomes counterproductive. The only difference is the level of arousal at which the fine line occurs. This relationship is illustrated in Figure 9.2.

On the whole, when an activity requires gross, overt movements in short, powerful bursts, it demands higher levels of arousal. On the other hand, when an activity requires refined, subtle movements or long-term sustained movements, it demands low levels of arousal.

Arousal curves are helpful in showing the physiological energy needs of an activity; however, they do not clearly show the individual performer's unique reactions to these situations. Every coach, supervisor, or teacher knows that the appropriateness of the arousal varies from performer to performer. For example, before a game, one football lineman

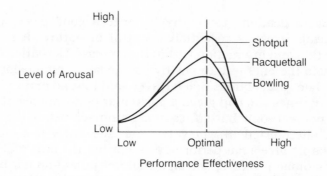

High

Level of Arousal

Low

Low   Optimal   High

Shotput

Racquetball

Bowling

Performance Effectiveness

Figure 9.2 A comparison of arousal curves for varying activities.

may need to bounce himself off a locker while another may need to relax, one musician may need to banter with friends while another may need to meditate, or one racquetball player may need to become angry while another may need to stretch.

A knowledge of how one is most appropriately aroused is critical in performing well, but this knowledge is incomplete unless it is viewed in relation to how one uniquely reacts and interacts with the pressures of the situation.

Stress

Stress is one of those "in" words most of us never heard until about 15 years ago. Then the media latched on to it, and we were bombarded with stories about stress. It was like waking up one morning and saying, "Oh, my goodness, I've got stress" (as if catching it in the night air!).

Although the word is relatively new, the concept it represents is not. Stress represents our perception of our abilities (or inabilities) to handle change and pressure. Too often we think of stress as being associated with negative situations, but any of you who have ever gone through a wedding, bought a house, had a child, or started a new job can attest that stress also occurs in seemingly happy events.

Some level of stress is necessary for performance as well. We need the stress of a busy intersection to energize us to cross, the stress of a sales meeting to energize us to present well, or some of us even need the stress of a night before a deadline to creatively write a good piece. Like arousal, stress is essentially neutral in nature. It is our reaction and interaction within that stressful situation that directs the energy into positive or negative dimensions.

The great actress Helen Hayes said that no matter how many times she had given a particular performance, if she did not feel some butterflies in her stomach before the first act, she started to worry because she knew she would probably give a flat performance. For her the butterflies in her stomach were a good sign that her mind and her body were preparing for a significant outlay of performance energies.

We can also react to stress in very negative ways. Headaches, ulcers, sleep problems, anger, eating problems, anxiety attacks, lethargy, apathy, and confusion are just some common examples. Basically, negative reactions to stressful situations emanate from an imbalance between our perception of the demands placed upon us and our perceived response capabilities. And when there is any kind of negative response or perceived imbalance to these stressful situations, our performances are likely to suffer.

State and trait stress. One way to better understand stress is to break it down into its two major elements. The first is called state stress which includes those pressures exerted on the performer within a specific situation. A particular recital, business presentation, or championship game contains many pressures and possible distractions. To say that the stress is not there is to lie to yourself and to rob yourself of a valuable source of energy.

Often, performers faced with the same pressures react differently to the stresses presented in a particular situation. Where one performer blooms, the other wilts. This type of stress is based on the performer's typical reaction to classes of pressurized situations and is called trait stress. It is what makes each performer unique. A Pete Rose, Mikhail Baryshnikov, or Lee Iacocca appear to thrive on the stress that stifles others in their respective fields.

For the most part, you do not have control over the causes of state stress because these are energies outside of your sphere of influence. Although you cannot control them, you can learn to better cope with these pressurized situations. Experience is a valuable teacher. If you have been in a similar situation before, the chances are that you can more quickly adapt to the stress than if you were experiencing it for the first time. On the other hand, you can adapt your level of trait stress by learning (or relearning) to manage your stress according to the particular situation. By taking the time to develop new patterns in your behavior, you will learn appropriate habits and unlearn the inappropriate ones. Acquiring a more adaptive stress level takes time, but it is something over which you can have control

Viewing stress in terms of state and trait is a handy way of recognizing which forms of stress you can and cannot control. Remember, even for those stressors you cannot control, you do have control of your reactions to them. This realization is the first step of standing apart from your peers in handling pressure.

Regression under stress.   An interesting phenomenon that many of us have experienced is called regression under stress. During pressurized performance situations, our skills (especially the more subtle and complicated ones) almost mysteriously disappear, so we regress to more simple and basic skill levels. For example, a tennis player who easily hits topspin backhands down the line in practice may discover that in pressurized situations he or she can only chop at the ball. A competent computer programmer may find that when the pressure is on to create a new program, he or she makes many simple mistakes and cannot think clearly. A golfer who sinks every 6-foot putt on the practice green finds that during the round he or she cannot get within 2 feet of the hole with the same 6-foot putt. Or a well-practiced pianist may find that during a recital the only thing he or she feels capable of playing is "Chopsticks"!

The phenomenon of regression under stress can provide an explanation for the "practice player." Everyone has probably known a performer who, after being outstanding in practice or rehearsal, looked like a beginner in the actual performance. Those people who have a high level of trait stress are more susceptible to state stress; hence, they regress to lower skill levels during the performances, where they are placed under greater state stress.

What causes this regression? Performers are more aroused in stressful situations, and if they are not used to performing in them, the only skills that can flow out are the more basic skills. The more advanced and refined skills are blocked by stress, and the overall performance suffers. Thus, the counterproductive forms of stress have overt and covert effects upon us. If we are not able to control our reactions to a pressurized situation, the stresses will sabotage our physical skills and subsequent confidence levels.

Then how do you do anything about it? As in talking about fear, many tryers become wrapped up in talking about stress. Indeed, these issues must first be addressed and explored to gain better understanding, but after a point, talking too much about them only promotes more fear and stress. The best way to begin learning how to handle and channel your performance energies is through relaxation.

Relaxation

If asked to choose just one factor on which to base good efforts, many performers, coaches, and teachers would select relaxation. Relaxation is one of the cornerstones of consistently high-level performances. Those who place great value on relaxation believe that (besides the direct benefits derived from it) if you can control yourself enough to relax, you can also exert the same control in your performances.

A relaxed state of mind prepares the performer to produce more effectively than if it were in a slightly tensed state, just as a relaxed muscle can contract more effectively than a slightly tensed one. Relaxation is nice in itself, but it also facilitates the organization of thoughts, conserves energy, heightens awareness, and controls minute aspects of a performance.

If you have ever witnessed an international track, wrestling, or weight lifting meet involving the Russians, you might have noticed how different they seemed before their events as compared to their Western counterparts. While the Western athletes might have been quite energized, boisterous, or even agitated, the Russians always seemed to be relaxed, calm, and even poised. In the 1920s the Russians led the world in the research of prestart tension and used these findings in training their athletes to relax and to conserve their energies (Vanek & Cratty, 1979). Then, once their performances began, they also learned how to unleash their energies in controlled and purposeful manners.

If I am overly fidgety before a performance, I am not only wasting precious energy, but I am also in less control of myself, especially of all my subtle motor skills; hence, I am more susceptible to regression under stress. Then as I begin my performance, I might start off slowly, make early mistakes, never find my optimal rhythms, or fade quickly.

As important as relaxation is, it must be seen as a tool to be used instead of an end in itself. Too many teachers, coaches, and even sports psychologists view relaxation as an end instead of a means to better control. These people mistakenly believe that all they have to do is relax and everything will proceed automatically; however, this is far from the case. Relaxation itself does not ensure a good performance, but very few good performances occur without relaxation. As with any skill, relaxation has to be used to achieve its best results.

Relaxation is the foundation of handling performance pressures and channeling your energies into productive directions. Staying relaxed keeps you at the helm of your performance ship. Once you are in your optimal performance zone, you are then better able to conserve, regulate, rechannel, and control all of your performance energies.

Types of Relaxation

Much of the reluctance many performers have in experimenting with and developing their own types of relaxation is that they become overwhelmed by the limitless number of approaches available. Those approaches that have either overly scientific or mystical connotations are simply unappealing. Many performers say, "I just want to learn how to relax. I don't want to become some kind of convert to a movement." When faced with the multitude of options, many people become even more tense and anxious!

On the whole, most performers already have a good deal of awareness and control over themselves. Hence, any form of relaxation they use will have quick and effective results. After experiencing how good it feels to really relax, most performers can see how these feelings are essential to any good performance.

Most styles of formal relaxation can be categorized as either cognitive (thinking) or somatic (feeling and sensing).

It does not matter which forms of relaxation you use. Although it would make sense to pair cognitive techniques with tension resulting from worries and somatic techniques with physical tension, some overlap of the techniques is common. Adopt the styles or portions of styles with which you feel most comfortable. The important thing is that you practice relaxation regularly. Autogenic training, biofeedback, transcendental meditation, other forms of meditation, Jacobsonian progressive relaxation, various styles of yoga, hypnosis, self-hypnosis, prayer, affirmations, mental imagery, zazen, and many other forms all achieve about the same brain wave states. They differ only in the paths they use to reach these brain wave states. No matter what you call it, relaxing is relaxing.

What most of these approaches have in common is their reliance on breathing. Deep, slow, and complete breathing seems to be a catalyst to relaxing and regulating the rest of the systems of the mind and body. McCluggage (1977) concluded that "you cannot experience anxiety unless you are breathing as if you were anxious" (p. 66). Taking this notion a little further, relaxation and tension are mutually exclusive. Relaxation, not anxiety or tension, is the natural state of the human being. (This may come as a surprise to stressed-out managers!) Given the opportunity, the body-mind will always return to its natural state of relaxation. The key is to give yourself the opportunity.

The effects of a relaxed state remain long after the relaxation process has ended. Murphy and White (1978) stated,

> In an old religious metaphor the act of meditation is compared to ringing a bell, in which the afterglow of the experience is like the dying sound. It is crucial to hit the bell (meditate again) before the ringing (the afterglow) stops. (p. 153)

Relaxing brings us back to our natural center of awareness. Pressures, anxieties, doubts, fears, distractions, and the like tend to draw us away from this center. Consistent relaxation not only brings us back to our center, but it also keeps us moving in the right direction from this center.

How to Relax

Before getting into the formal relaxation sequence, please do this little relaxation exercise: *Cover up the rest of the page after this paragraph.* To begin, wherever you are reading this, take a couple of moments to find a comfortable position. Now go on reading.

That's the exercise! Did you change your position? Most of you did. (Surely, this book isn't all that exciting that you have to sit on the edge of the seat chewing on every word!)

Those of you who did move, Were you aware of your discomfort? Probably not, or you would have adjusted your position before I gave you permission to do so. Most of us go through the day quite unaware of our bodies and the signals they send us. It usually isn't until these signals become very loud (in such forms as headaches or backaches) that we become aware of them. For example, I may be carrying a lot of tension in my shoulders for a couple of days. My shoulders may be in a constant state of semishrug, but if I am unaware, I might think that this is normal. If I don't listen to these signals from my shoulders, I may wake up one morning with a backache and then ask myself, "What did I do to myself yesterday that I got this backache?" It was not what I did to myself yesterday, but what I did to myself the previous 12 yesterdays (and was unaware of) that caused the backache.

Awareness is the x-ray of optimal performance. Once aware, I am able to make the adjustments in my body and in my performance form that will maximize my efforts. Awareness goes hand in hand with relaxation: The more relaxed I am, the more open the lines of communication between my mind and body. Concurrently, the more aware I am of myself, the more effectively I will be able to relax.

A basic relaxation sequence. The following is an elementary form of relaxation. If you do not have a regular relaxation exercise, experiment with this one. If you do have a regular format, pick and choose pieces of this one and integrate them into your existing style.

You may want to tape this or have a friend read it to you. In either case, speak with a soothing voice. Frequently pause during and after sentences. (I have suggested some pauses in the text.) If you are unsure about the pace, remember that it is better to go too slow than too fast.

Find a place where you won't be disturbed for about 15 minutes. Close the door, take the phone off the hook, and tell the kids not to disturb you. Next, take off as much clothing as you are comfortable with. Especially make sure to loosen any belts or garments that constrict the waist. Take out your contact lenses if your eyes become irritated when they are closed for over 10 minutes. If you lie down, be sure to do so on your back because there is more supporting structure there. Whether you sit or lie down, make sure your arms and legs are uncrossed, because when crossed, they minutely yet significantly restrict the blood flow to the lower parts.

Here we go!

When you are ready to, close your eyes and become aware of your presence in this room. . . . (5-second pause). Now that your eyes are closed . . . (3-second pause), start tuning into some of your other senses beginning with your sense of hearing. . . . Ask yourself what kinds of sounds you hear. Outside the room . . . inside the room . . . within yourself. . . . Recognize that during the course of this, some sounds may distract you or your mind may wander. If any of these occur, fine. Just catch yourself, come back on course, and go on. All of us become distracted at times. And all of our minds wander at times. The important thing is to go back on course. . . .

Now tune into your sense of smell and note any subtle odors or fragrances. . . . Now tune into your sense of taste and note anything you can taste. How much saliva is there? You may want to feel your taste buds more by rubbing your tongue against the roof of your mouth. . . .

Finally, tune into your general body sensations. . . . Note how relatively hot or cold the room is for you. What parts of your body are warmer or colder than other parts? . . . What parts of your body are in contact with the chair (or floor or bed)? . . . You may even feel some air passage brushing against your cheeks or arms. . . .

As you tune into your body, you may want to adjust your position in order to become even more comfortable. Now look for sources of tension, tightness, fatigue, or pain in your body. . . . When you find a place, gently move it and let the tension go. . . . There is no need to keep it tight. . . . If you are unsure whether or not a place is tense, experiment with tensing and relaxing that spot in order to feel the difference when it is tensed . . . and when it is relaxed. . . .

Scan down from your scalp . . . to your forehead . . . to your jaw . . . to your throat and neck . . . to your shoulders . . . and down your arms to your hands. . . . Good. . . . Now, scan through your chest, feeling your ribcage expanding and sinking. . . . Work your way around to your upper back and slowly feel each vertebra as you work your way down your spine. . . . You may already be experiencing that the areas you have scanned have become more relaxed on their own. They may feel looser . . . warmer . . . or heavier. . . .

Continue your scanning by becoming aware of your abdomen . . . your hips . . . your buttocks . . . the back of your thighs (hamstrings) . . . the front of your thighs (quadriceps) . . . your knees . . . shins . . . calves . . . ankles . . . and feet . . . so that you have scanned the entire length of your body. . . .

Good. . . . Now, shift your attention to your breathing. Don't change it . . . just passively observe it. . . . Follow the path your breathing takes as it goes in your nose . . . down your throat . . . and out again. . . . Allow yourself to ride the crest of your breathing . . . (10-second pause).

You might wish to imagine that your breathing is like gentle little waves washing upon a shore. As you breathe in . . . the wave comes in . . . and as your breathe out . . . the wave leaves. . . . See this scene. . . . Feel it. . . . Each time you breathe out—each time the wave leaves—it seems to wash away more and more tension, tightness, and extraneous thoughts from you. . . . You might even feel this tension or tightness being gently washed away and leaving through your fingers or toes. . . .

Good. . . . Now allow your breathing to change so that it becomes very slow . . . very deep . . . and very complete. . . . Breathe just fast enough so you don't feel the need to gasp for air. . . . Breathe slowly so that it takes you 3 . . . 4 . . . even 5 seconds to inhale . . . and as much time to exhale. . . . Very slow . . . very deep . . . and very complete. . . .

As your breathing slows . . . feel some of your other systems slowing down as well. . . . Heart rate slowing . . . thinking slowing . . . blood pressure dropping . . . digestive system slowing. . . . So that all of you . . . is slowing down. . . .

You may already have started to feel yourself sinking into the chair (or couch or bed). . . . Now, with each relaxing exhale . . . you can actually feel yourself sinking further and further into the chair. . . . Sinking further and further . . . into being relaxed. . . .

Just let yourself drift . . . and enjoy the feeling of being more . . . and more . . . relaxed . . . (10-second pause).

Good. . . . Now I am going to count back from 4 to 1 . . . and when I reach 1, you can open your eyes. . . .

Here we go. . . . 4, (gently raise your voice here) your awareness is coming back into this room . . . back to your senses. . . . 3, you are feeling very relaxed and refreshed. . . . As we reach 2, start moving around a little. . . . moving your head and arms, shrugging your shoulders, and stretching like a cat. . . . And now take a couple of final deep breaths . . . and 1. . . .

Stretch and look around. Notice the differences in the ways you feel now compared with before you started. Most of you will feel more relaxed. There may be parts of you that still feel tense or tight. That's okay. It may take several more times through the exercise to allow those parts to relax. In some cases, it took years for those parts to become tight, so it makes sense that it might take awhile to have them return to a more relaxed state.

How long did it seem that you had your eyes closed? For most of you, it would have seemed significantly shorter or longer than the actual time. This is because through relaxation we tune more into our own internal clocks instead of outside objective time.

If you fell asleep, that's okay. It is probably what you needed to do. If you continue to fall asleep during this exercise, do it earlier in the day. Also, before you start the relaxation, tell yourself that you will stay awake. Most of all, don't worry about it.

Note how long the feelings of relaxation last. For most of us, these feelings last somewhere between 15 minutes and 3 hours. As you know how long you stay relaxed, you can then plan another sequence when the feelings are wearing off.

Do this exercise at least twice a day: once in the morning and once in the afternoon. Do not wait until evening to do it. By that time the damage from the stresses of the day have already been done, and anything you do will have minimal effects. It is your challenge to work this exercise into your daily routine. You will quickly discover that relaxing also has a rejuvenating effect so that it allows you to pace and extend yourself better throughout your day.

Some hints.   One of your goals in learning how to relax is to develop your own unique style of relaxing. There are many good sources that can provide you with excellent examples of different styles of relaxing. Some of the best are marked with an asterisk in the bibliography under the heading "Relaxation and Visualization." Use these sources, audiotapes, or the relaxation script just presented as catalysts in developing your own unique style of relaxing. Do not become dependent on them (e.g., "I can't relax now because the batteries in my tape recorder are dead") because you are then abdicating your responsibility and control for self to some external source. Currently, I use about 13 different forms of relaxing with my clients. By introducing so many forms, my clients have the opportunity to pick and choose those aspects of each they like and integrate them into their own unique styles.

Here are some more specific hints in employing relaxation. First, you must set a priority to your relaxing. If you say to yourself, "Well, I'll relax when I find the time today," we all know that you will never find the time. Set aside times in your daily schedule to relax. Second, the times when you feel you have the least amount of time to relax are the times when you need it the most. When you find yourself saying, "I don't have time to relax now. I've got to do this and this and this," are the times you really need to relax because those are the times when you are the most stressed and fragmented. Finally, experiment with your relaxing before a practice or rehearsal. After a while, you may be able to relax with your eyes open and even incorporate it into your stretching, warm-up, or set-up routine.

Relaxing is a skill that like any other skill will take time to develop and refine. And like any other skill, the more proficient you become with your own unique style, the less time it will take to become more deeply relaxed. The key is to regularly practice your own style of relaxing.

The more often you relax, the better you will be able to see (and feel) the benefits, and the more it will become a regular part of your life. Relaxing will quickly progress from a need to a want to a "gotta" (as in, "I just gotta relax now"). Relaxing will eventually become so desirable that it will actually be more distressing not to do it! So go do it . . . and enjoy!

Channeling Energy Into Performances

Relaxation is nice in itself, and it also provides a base from which people can better control and channel their energies into their performances. This is a greater challenge than most people realize. You see, it is relatively easy to relax in a nice comfortable setting. The real challenge comes in learning how to apply these relaxation principles in pressurized performance situations. In this section the major issues and approaches helpful in applying relaxation skills in performing situations will be explored.

An important principle of high-level performing is to realize that energy is energy, whatever its shape and form. Once this is understood, the goal in handling any counterproductive energy is *not* to get rid of it, for then you are losing precious energy. You are, so to speak, cutting off your performance nose to spite your performance face. Rather, the goal in handling any counterproductive energy is to rechannel this energy into productive directions. For example, a little prestart tension and anxiety is good, but too much impedes the performance. Instead of trying to get rid of this energy, you must learn how to rechannel it back into your energy reservoir so that it can later be used positively in the performance.

Energy Exchange

Most of us have learned that in any interaction, communication occurs simultaneously at two levels. The first level is the verbal information level. The second level is an energy exchange level where you can sense the other person's feelings. Those of you who have ever been in a customer service occupation can attest to the existence of this second level. There were times when a customer came through the door that you sensed he was loaded for bear. (If you were smart, you would take your break then!) Even before he started talking, you could sense his energy. The same kind of energy exchange occurs in performances, and people need to be aware of its existence. As they do, they will have a whole extra dimension in which to operate.

State stress infers that there is always some kind of energy exchange between the performer and the environment. These exchanges can be positive (e.g., inspirations derived from a cheering crowd) or negative (e.g., distractions or pessimism from teammates). Too often we allow negative, disruptive, or distracting influences from the environment to tap into and sap our performance energies. Although we do not have control over these influences, we can learn how to appropriately react to them so that our efforts remain effectively directed.

Those of you who have studied any form of martial arts know that those practices are as much an exercise of energy exchange as they are of physical technique. If I am 5 ft 2 in. and someone 6 ft 8 in. comes rushing at me, it would be foolish to meet him head-on. The martial arts teach me how to deflect this energy so that my opponent assumes a weaker position, while I assume a stronger position so that I can either dismiss or throw him.

This "mental aikido" can be employed in everyday life. When I was a novice psychotherapist, I used to be drained at the end of the day from listening to all the grief, anger, fear, and anxiety of my clients. I eventually discovered that besides the verbal communication, an energy exchange was always going on between us during the session. From this realization I developed the mental technique that whenever a client was throwing out this negative energy, I would visualize this energy going out the window! This was my mental escape valve. I sometimes even visualized this energy going into my garbage can or into my flower pots. (Boy, did I have green plants!) Doing this did not mean that I was insensitive or uncaring. On the contrary, deflecting this negative energy kept me in a better position to retain the perspectives I needed to be genuinely helpful.

On those occasions when I did somehow allow this disruptive energy to land on me, another simple technique I employed was to simply shrug my shoulders. As I shrugged, I visualized myself casting off this negative energy. I also said things to myself such as, "I don't know," "I'll cross that bridge if and when I get to it," "Hey, I screwed up," "That's okay," "I forgive myself," "It is his problem and not mine," or "I am doing the best job I can." Shrugging not only kept those huge muscles of my shoulders, neck, and upper back loose, it also helped me to maintain perspective. Again, shrugging off the negative energy was not being caustic, cynical, or indifferent; rather, it was an approach to keep me aware and positively responsive to my environment.

Performers can use these two energy exchange techniques in almost any pressurized situation. For example, when you make a mistake, shrug your shoulders. When there is a lot of potentially distracting crowd or media attention, visualize yourself sidestepping this attention and seeing it going past you. When you feel the pressures of an important point or sequence, shrug your shoulders, say something reassuring to yourself, and smile. When a prospect is asking you a lot of tough questions, turn this energy around in your mind, realizing that if he or she were not interested, he or she would not be taking the time to ask these questions. Finally, when you give a presentation to your bosses, visualize your pressures flying out the window. There are many more applications for these two techniques; your challenge is to remember to use them.

Transferring Into Performance Situations

The techniques mentioned above are gimmicks, nothing more. Their purpose is to return you to your states of relaxation and control. This implies, however, that you must have been relaxed and in control in the first place.

After you have developed your own unique style of relaxing, you must then discover when it is most effectively employed prior to a performance. Some people find they need to relax on the morning of the performance, others wait until they have arrived at the performance arena, still others need to relax right up to the start of their performance. Listen to yourself early in your performance for signals indicating whether or not you are in your optimal performance zone. No matter the performance specialty, there is always a tendency to go too fast, push too much, and try too hard early in the performance. Relax, slow down, and listen to yourself.

Anger, fear, and anxiety are all indications that you are out of control. Slow down, shrug your shoulders, and even laugh at yourself! The last thing you need here is to be more intense. Pause, follow your breathing, and focus on what specific things you need to do.

Anxiety and worry sap precious energy, so pace yourself during the performance. Avoid the temptation of expending all your energy at the beginning. Remember, it is more enjoyable to end your performance on a high note than to barely survive it. If you are being evaluated, recognize that the last thing you do is usually the first thing your critics remember. By pacing yourself and conserving your energy early, you can end your performance on a crescendo.

If you are feeling fatigued or are losing your concentration late in the performance and if you have the opportunity, take a relaxation break. During this time attempt to both revitalize yourself as well as achieve the same relaxed feelings with which you started. If you do not have the opportunity to take a break, really concentrate, conserve what energy you have left, and push yourself. The quality of your efforts here may be as important as the results, for you will prove to yourself that you can endure during the tough times.

Throughout your performance, focus and channel your mental and physical energies into doing well those things you need to do. Distractions, fears, anxieties, pessimism, and ill-defined objectives all sap energy. Do not channel your energies away from those things you must not do because then you are only emphasizing them; rather, continually channel all your energies toward the things you need to do.

All this channeling and focusing is dependent on control. And control is dependent on relaxation. Get used to relaxing in and out of performance situations. Not only will you find it enjoyable, you will also find that it is the keystone for mastery. The ability to relax cannot be over-emphasized. It is the foundation on which more advanced mental processes rest. Two of these processes will be further explored in the next two chapters on mental imagery and self-statements.

Chapter 9 Performance Skills

- Energy is life. We need to be aware of it, to conserve it, and to control it. With regards to performance, we have to understand which forms of energy impede us as well as what we can do about them.

- Energy is neutral. How we use or abuse it in different situations is what makes it positive or negative. So the goal in viewing any kind of performance energy is not to get rid of it, but to channel it into productive directions.

- The two major components of performance energy are arousal and stress. Arousal is a state during which our bodies are superenergized and our minds are super-focused. There is, however, a point at which any additional arousal will only serve to inhibit performance.

- Stress is your mind's and body's reaction to change, any kind of change. State stress is that stress associated with the performance situation; trait stress is that stress associated with an individual's unique personality responses.

- Relaxing is the key in handling performance pressures. Develop your own unique style(s) of relaxing and learn how to apply your formal as well as informal techniques to your performance situations.

- Relaxation is enjoyable in itself, and it also serves as a base from which you can channel, direct, and control your efforts. Learn to relax for both purposes.

- Notes: _____

  _____

  _____

  _____

  _____

- Additions or changes to your personal performance formula:

  _____

  _____

  _____

  _____

chapter 10

The Mind's Eye

*You are never given a wish without also being given
the power to make it come true. You may have to
work for it, however.*
—Richard Bach

One resource for channeling our performance energies
more effectively is mental imagery. The applications of
mental imagery have become increasingly refined and
sophisticated. As we used to rely on wishing, hoping, and
willpower, we are now replacing them with precise forms of
mental imagery such as monitoring imagery, self-regulating
visualizations, and mental rehearsal.

The Realms of Imagery

Mental imagery itself is not new; it has been used
throughout history in various symbolic, healing, religious,
and artistic ways. The newness lies in the ways imagery can
be structured so that it can be applied to very specific
purposes, including improving performance. Writing in a
preface (Samuels & Samuels, 1975), Don Gerrard summarized,

> If there are two important "new" concepts of the 20th Century
> American life, they are meditation and visualization. Meditation
> clears and concentrates the mind; visualization puts an image
> in it which can profoundly affect the life. (p. xi)

Relaxing, centering, or meditating is the clay that forms our
aspirations. Mental imagery is the tool that shapes, refines,
and actualizes these aspirations.

Today, mental imagery is employed in such varied pursuits as healing and health, psychotherapy, creativity, dreamwork, problem solving, strategic planning, parapsychology, learning and retention, monitoring and self-regulation, personal growth, and of course, performance. The applications are about as numerous and varied as the mind can imagine!

In our daily lives we rely more on mental imagery than we are aware. We may visualize how we are going to look with a particular combination of clothes when we are choosing them in the morning, or we may visualize how the living room is going to look before we rearrange the furniture. Many of us may rehearse what we are going to say in an upcoming conversation, or we may visualize how a word looks when we are figuring out how to spell it. And when we are working through a problem, most of us "try on for size" possible solutions. Our uses of mental imagery have become so automatic that few of us realize how much we really use it.

Images precede words. Mental imagery taps into portions of the conscious that the verbal, quantitative, and analytical parts of our brains rarely reach. The processes of constructing concepts and words are extremely complicated and require the highest levels of the brain. Mental imagery employs relatively lower levels of the brain and, as such, is not under the direct conscious control of the higher levels. Dreams, flashes of insight, daydreams, fantasies, and even hallucinations are some examples of mental imagery that are rarely controlled by our rational minds.

Physiologically, mental imagery is similar to actual visual perception. Samuels & Samuels (1975) stated, "It has been found that mental images have many of the same physical components as open-eyed perceptions" (p. 57). For example, when we close our eyes and vividly imagine some kind of scene, action, or experience, our eyes move as if the action were actually occurring. So there are many actual and metaphorical parallels between mental imagery and visual perception. It is because of this parallel that so many visual words accurately describe the various processes of mental imagery.

Our everyday phrases are another indication of how much we rely on mental imagery. "Seeing with the mind's eye," "movies of the mind," "envisioning success," "imagine that," "picture this," and even, "I see" are some typical examples. If you were to keep a list of such visual phrases for a few days, you would be surprised at how many similar phrases you discover.

When words stop, images resume. There are only about 350,000 words in the English language. This is a relatively small number considering the myriad of combinations of concepts, feelings, and experiences they must convey. Mental imagery is a supplemental way of formulating and expressing these concepts. Without mental imagery our experiences and communications would be extremely limited.

Some people cannot see in mental pictures, but they usually can employ other forms of mental imagery. These people can use auditory (hearing) imagery or kinesthetic (body sensation) imagery to replace or supplement the visual imagery. We not only have our five senses, but the brain also has its corresponding mental senses it uses to understand, solve problems, and create. Many of us can *feel* the warm sand between our toes on a beach even if we are hundreds of miles away from it, can *smell* the fragrance of a rose even in the winter, can *hear* the sweet complexities of a Mozart symphony, or can *taste* the sourness of a lemon. So you do not have to be visual to utilize mental imagery. If you cannot visualize, shift whatever I say about images into the internal sensing dimension that works for you.

Very little of mental imagery can be called magical or mystical. Instead, mental imagery has become a practical and effective tool for facilitating development in all areas of our lives. One of the newest and most exciting of these areas is mental imagery's applications in improving performance. These various applications of mental imagery will be explored in this chapter. We will look at the major types of mental imagery and how they are specifically utilized in performance and then present a step-by-step sequence of how they can be employed.

Spacing Out and Tuning In

Mental imagery can be divided into two general forms. The first form is used to "space out" from oneself or from a given place and time. This form is called disassociative imagery. The second form is used to "tune into" oneself more specifically. This form is called associative imagery. Let's explore each of these in more detail and see how they can be used in performance.

Disassociative Imagery[1]

One of the most common uses of disassociative imagery is a kind of mental anaesthesia that serves to take one's mind off the problems or discomforts at hand. Daydreaming, creating a pleasant scene, reliving a nice memory, or simply spacing out are forms of this kind of imagery. For example, when I am in the dentist's chair, I am usually creating a pleasant scene (either one I have physically been in before, an imaginary one, or a combination of both) that will serve to disassociate me from that given moment. Beyond that, I am actually *in* that pleasant scene. So when the drill is whirling, I don't hear (or feel) it because I am on the beaches at Tahiti! This form of imagery is called disassociative because it *dis-associates* me to a more internal and self-controlled state of consciousness. The disassociative imagery can be employed to temporarily avoid reality (e.g., the dentist's drill) or to relive a pleasant memory.

Disassociative imagery can be used as a catalyst to create a kind of mental blank screen in which additional receptive images can appear. This receptive imagery is most often used in creativity, problem solving, brainstorming, and healing. Creative people often allow their minds to wander in order to explore new perspectives or variations. These new perspectives or variations take the form of receptive images on the blank screens of their conscious awareness.

Innovative problem solvers are frequently known for their abilities to incubate, or sleep on a problem. Solutions from these deeper levels of consciousness most often present themselves in the forms of images. The most famous example of this is the chemist Kekule's symbolic image of a snake biting its own tail, which stimulated his conception of the benzene ring.

[1]I prefer to use the word *disassociate* instead of *dissociate* because the latter word can have more psychopathological, psychoanalytical, and even chemical connotations. Also, for me, *disassociation* is more aesthetically compatible with its counterpart *association* than is *dissociation*.

Unique approaches to healing—especially with cancer, flu, and viruses—are often inspired by receptive images that represent the healing processes. Images of white knights killing dragons, good fish eating bad fish, golden cleansing fluids, swirling brushes, and more recently, Pac Man-like figures devouring dots are the typical examples of visual representations of healing.

Disassociative imagery can also be stimulated by sounds, especially music. When hearing an old song, most of us have experienced the phenomenon of going back in time to the situation or circumstance where we first heard it. Another example where sound facilitates disassociating imagery can be found on the local running path. The headphones runners wear distract them from the discomforts of running by helping them space out or create pleasant scenes on the movie screens of their minds.

Although most disassociative imagery is by choice (from some level of consciousness), it can also be derived as a function of physiological changes during a long activity. Endurance athletes are frequently known to experience disassociative images that are the results of greater amounts of endorphins (a kind of natural morphinelike secretion) in the brain during prolonged activity. This is most often referred to as the runner's high, and although much of the popularization of this phenomenon has been discredited, there are definite alterations in consciousness that can cause various mental images within endurance athletes.

Disassociative imagery is pleasant in itself, and it also serves as a base for associative imagery. To best associate I must first clear my mind of all the clutter. Disassociative imagery is that mental broom that housecleans the mind so that it can effectively associate.

Associative Imagery

Associative forms of mental imagery function to tune into one's body and mind. Just as tuning a radio makes the reception more clear, so does tuning into the body-mind make interpreting its signals and its subsequent control more precise and effective.

Associative imagery is most often referred to as visualization. Visualization is controlled and directed imagery that can be used for awareness building, monitoring and self-regulation, healing, and even as a kind of mental programming for good performances. Visualization entails controlling the image and directing it to the desired positive results. Whether the mental scenario be healing a pulled calf muscle, executing precise school figures, or recalling the outline of a presentation, visualization facilitates the integration and mobilization of all one's mental and physical resources.

One factor that seems to differentiate elite and world class athletes from very good or recreational ones is that the elite athletes continually associate with themselves, whereas the good or recreational ones are more apt to dissassociate. Elite marathoners more often monitor themselves so that they can quickly detect and effectively adjust to the changes occurring within them. In contrast, recreational marathoners have the tendency to space out to avoid the discomfort. Prima ballerinas more often listen to their bodies, searching for signs of fatigue or strain so that they can correct themselves before an injury occurs. Secondary ballerinas, however, are more apt to allow themselves to be distracted by external events so that they are less aware of approaching injuries. Olympian bodybuilders rely on what is called the instinctive training principle where they design their daily workouts by scanning how they feel that day. Recreational bodybuilders usually listen to loud music and do the same routines mindlessly for months on end.

Visualizing associates, or involves me more, with my mind and body. If I am unaware of the subtle changes occurring within me, how can I adjust to them? When I am less aware of myself, it isn't until an injury takes on more traumatic proportions or the contest has slipped away that I realize the adjustments I should have made earlier. Visualization, then, serves a threefold purpose: It facilitates awareness, it promotes control and aids adjustments, and it facilitates preparation by programming the specific mental and physical skills.

Both disassociative and associative imagery are necessary in high-level performances. The key is to know just when to apply each. There are times when I may wish to disassociate and let my imagination run wild. These disassociative images may be pleasant escapes, or they may indirectly be used to aid in problem solving or in creating. However, there are other times when I may need to associate in order to regulate, heal, or mentally rehearse my performance. Both forms give me important tools to maximize the powers of my mind.

The Applications of Mental Imagery

The applications of mental imagery in performance range from the remedial to the preventative to the developmental. We can use mental imagery to help heal injuries, to monitor ourselves so that we prevent injuries, and to promote high-level performances. The major categories of these applications fall under the classifications of healing, monitoring and self-regulation, and process imagery.

Healing

The specialization known as sports medicine has taken quantum leaps during the last decade. What used to be treated only by a crusty yet sympathetic trainer with a rubdown is now increasingly approached with a myriad of machines, techniques, and specialists. As the sophistication of sports medicine grew, one factor became increasingly evident: Performers have to take more active responsibilities in their own healing.

By all estimates, modern medicine only touches about 10% of what can be called health. The rest is covered by factors that are outside the domain of formalized medicine. Heredity, environmental factors, nutrition, exercise, chemical abuses, attitudes, stress and relationships comprise most of the factors that influence an individual's health.

In all forms of medicine the role of the passive patient is falling by the wayside. It has been found that if people were more involved in the healing of their injuries and illnesses, they would be more apt to be involved in all aspects of their health. One approach that not only facilitates healing, but also promotes a greater sense of self-responsibility is visualization.

Much of the knowledge of the uses of visualization in the healing of sports injuries has been adopted from work with severely ill or terminal patients. The works of the Simontons (1978) and Jampolsky (1979) showed that structured visualization techniques can aid in reducing pain, supplement the natural healing processes, and give the individual a greater sense of control.

In sports medicine, visualization is used in two general ways: visualizing the healing processes and visualizing the final healed state. For example, if I have a strained quadriceps muscle, I might visualize such healing processes as the muscle fibers loosening and realigning, healing warmth pervading the muscle, or little antibodies in the forms of tiny masseuses mending the muscle. Better yet, in conjunction with a whirlpool or massage, I might visualize the damaged cells being washed away or the striations being soothed. Finally, I would visualize the desired states of a healed and healthy quadriceps muscle as being firm, cool, elastic, smooth, red, dense, vibrant, bright, or solid.

Although one must individualize the healing visualizations to fit the unique situations, I like to use Samuels and Bennett's (1974) visual guidelines for healing processes and healed states.

Basic healing processes:

- *erasing bacteria or viruses*
- *building new cells to replace damaged ones*
- *making rough areas smooth*
- *making hot areas cool*
- *making tense areas relax*
- *draining swollen areas*
- *releasing pressure from tight areas*
- *bringing blood to areas that need nutrients*
- *bringing blood to areas that need to be cleansed*
- *making areas that are too wet drier*
- *making areas that are too dry wetter*
- *bringing energy to areas that seem fatigued*

Basic sensations of healed states:

- *smoothness*
- *comfort*
- *gentle warmth*

- *the suppleness of new tissue*
- *moistness (not too wet, not too dry)*
- *resiliency*
- *strength*
- *ease and harmony*

(pp. 143-145)

Consistent and creative uses of visualization do seem to accelerate the healing of sport- and performance-related injuries. However, we must remember that visualization is a supplement to the other more established healing approaches; it is *not* a substitute for them. Visualization should be learned and practiced under the supervision of a trained professional so that athletes and performers do not have misconceptions about being healed when they are actually still injured. Two additional benefits of using visualization in healing are that performers learn the basics of effective visualization and that they gain a greater sense of self-responsibility. These two lessons can be carried over to aid them in the improvement of their performances after they have recovered.

Monitoring and Self-Regulation

Monitoring and self-regulation go hand in hand. The awareness I use to scan by body for signals of fatigue or pain is the same awareness I use in making the necessary adjustments. Elite endurance athletes make numerous adjustments during a long event. Factors such as posture, form, rhythm and tempo, stride, footplant, and pace must stay constantly in tune with the state the performer is in at any given time.

Visualization is an essential component to these monitoring and self-regulating processes. Do you remember the old *Star Trek* series? You may wish to apply some of their terminology in monitoring yourself. *Scan* and use your *sensors* to become more aware of the various parts of your body. For example, right now scan your left biceps muscle. Picture it in your mind's eye. Scan up and down, across, and into this muscle. If you are having trouble scanning it, physically tense and relax your left biceps muscles so you feel their extremes. Now add to this picture how they feel.

Next, add the colors and textures of this muscle. As you become more aware of your left biceps, zoom in your picture so that you visualize all the muscle fibers. Don't worry if your picture is not anatomically correct. The important thing is to develop a precise picture of your image of your left biceps.

Most of you had varying degrees of success with this scanning. For some of you the best you could attain was a general feeling of the muscle. Others might have been able to visualize the striations. The ability to use visualization in such monitoring is like focusing a microscope: Some of you might be at the level of using the coarse adjustment knob, while others might be at the level of using the fine adjustment knob. Practice will bring refinement.

As you become more accurate in your monitoring, you will be more able to detect any changes in your body. Visualization can also be applied to adjusting to these changes, which is called self-regulation. Self-regulation is a more active involvement with your body and your performance efforts so that you can stay aligned with your most natural (hence, optimal) levels of functioning. Shealy (1976) has employed many forms of visualization in healing. Included are some examples I have used of variations of those visualizations that can be specifically applied to self-regulation during performing.

At the beginning of a run when I have monitored and noticed that my hamstrings are tight, I visualize that my nostrils are *in* my hamstrings! I create a very specific picture of my nostrils functioning from my hamstrings and use all of my mental senses to develop this picture. After that, I visualize breathing in and out *through* my hamstrings, feeling the energy exchange taking place through my hamstrings. Each time I inhale through my hamstrings, I feel fresh energy coming in, and each time I exhale, I feel the stiffness and tightness leaving.

As the run progresses, I visualize my heart beating at a slow, methodical, and efficient pace. (It does not matter whether or not I can feel my actual heart beat.) Along with this visualization, I also hear an imaginary, constant sound (much like the mantra *Om* or like the dull hum of a finely tuned engine) that represents the efficient rhythm of my running.

As I sense fatigue, I shake my hands or kick up my heels for a couple of strides and, at the same time, visualize the fatigue leaving my body through my shaking hands or kicking heels. Feeling the fatigue leaving, I become rejuvenated.

Near the end of the run when my monitoring detects some tightness in my calves, I visualize rich, red, cool blood (warm blood on cold days) pulsating through my calves. I know that this imagery pulsating is bringing refreshing oxygen to my calves and washing away the tightness.

These are just some examples of self-regulating visualizations.

Process Imagery

As the title implies, process imagery involves those pictures that emerge and are created during the actual practices and performances. These images can come from both disassociative and associative states. They are images that are initially unplanned but can subsequently be applied to enhance future efforts.

Quite often a simple image can effectively replace words, concepts, or conscious thoughts. For instance, imagine this scene: You are swimming and a piano falls on your back! This accurately describes how sprint swimmers often feel when they tire during the latter portions of a race. They relate that they tired so dramatically on that last length that it was if a piano had fallen on their backs. No further words are necessary to describe this state!

Business people are increasingly employing a variety of process visualizations in their daily work settings. Some leaders visualize their organizations to be a great animal or machine with each unit or worker representing a specific characteristic. Innovative salespeople greatly rely on process visualizations. They are open to such visualizations coming to them during their sales presentations which they transform into metaphors to help them communicate more effectively. Many even try to get the prospect to visualize how it would feel to have their product or service. Process visualizations enhance many athletes' efforts (performances) as well.

Arnold Schwarzenegger imagines—and subsequently routinely visualizes—that his biceps are mountain peaks that fill up the room when he exercises them. Many cross-country skiers, swimmers, bicyclists, race walkers, and runners frequently visualize that they are a kind of ship's bow or figurehead that effortlessly slices through the air, snow, or water. While ascending a hill, some runners and cross-country skiers also visualize themselves being pulled up by an invisible ski lift chair or rope. Dancers frequently visualize themselves floating through very complicated steps where their feet barely touch the floor. Gymnasts and figure skaters who train with a safety harness often visualize that they are still wearing it during their performances.

The process images of some sort of spring or coil are very prevalent among performers who rely on their legs or backs. Sprinters, long jumpers, dancers, platform divers, figure skaters, and high jumpers often see their legs as great springs that propel them. Discus throwers, shot putters, tennis players, golfers, and hammer throwers frequently visualize that their torsos are great coils that unleash themselves at their moments. Further, a great variety of performers often imagine themselves to be some kind of animal that represents all their optimal performing qualities.

What's Your Animal?

Most performance activites are so complicated and involve so many intricacies that it is often difficult and confusing for the performer to focus on all of them. The problem is that when a person focuses on one aspect, the other aspects of the activity usually suffer. Also, focusing on one aspect during the activity tends to plunge the performer into the thinking-while-doing trap.

Plan to spend about 15 minutes for this exercise. Sit down with a pad of paper in a quiet place and think back to your specific activity. Remember those performances in which everything went exceptionally well. Start writing down all those qualities, factors, aspects, components, and states of mind that contributed to those outstanding efforts. Be very specific.

Now reread them and see if any more come to mind. Write these down as well. Take your time. Some factors may stimulate other factors. Most of you will fill up at least one sheet of paper. It is not uncommon to list over 50 factors.

Next, close your eyes, relax, and let your mind drift. Focus on all the qualities you listed on the paper *as a whole.* Remember the feelings associated with these qualities. Gradually allow the image of an animal to come to you that represents all of your superperformance qualities. The animal can be real or imaginary. What does it look like? What color is it? What kind of texture does it have? How does it act? Use all of your inner senses to become familiar with your performing animal.

Now try to feel what it would be like to be the animal that represents all your positive performance qualities. *Become* this animal. If you were a runner, you might imagine yourself a panther and take on its strength, quickness, intelligence, and powerful kick. If you were a dancer, you might imagine you are an impala, full of grace and poise, yet still powerful and enduring. If you were a cross-country skier, you might imagine yourself the lionness with her sustained rhythm and speed. And in business, if you were a stockbroker, you might imagine yourself a bull or bear that reflects the prevailing position of the market. A businesswoman might imagine herself a feline or a combination of animals that represent flexibility in management.

Then let your image leave, and allow your mind to drift again. Gradually, return to reality and open your eyes.

At your next training, practice, or rehearsal session, instead of focusing on all those specific, complicated, and isolated qualities, simply ease off and *be* your animal! Knowing that this animal represents all of your superperformance qualities, allow yourself to become your animal. However, many of these animals may change with time. As one's event, position, mastery of skills, or understanding of self-change, so does the animal. Quite often the animal is further refined, becoming both more surrealistic, yet more accurate. Get to know your performance animal and become comfortable taking on its qualities.

Consistently high-level performers have learned to trust all these process images. They usually do not know from where these images came, but because they feel right, these people regularly use them. Look forward and be receptive to the images that occur to you during your performances. They are not only signs that you are on the right course, they are also tools that you can apply to make your efforts even more effective.

As the knowledge and refinement of mental imagery in performance increases, so does its sophistication. For over a decade I have been promoting mental imagery. Often viewed as being interesting, mental imagery has been considered more of a luxury. I now believe that if you are not regularly employing various forms of mental imagery, you are falling behind your colleagues who are.

Mental Rehearsal

Mental rehearsal is the state-of-the-art form of visualization that helps performers clarify, prepare, practice, refine, and attain their goals. Specifically, mental rehearsal involves proceeding through a sequence of events, vividly recalling the minute processes of training or performing and visualizing the desired results of those processes.

Mental rehearsal is not new; variations have been around for decades. Singer (1975) pointed out that "as far back as 1899, the question was raised whether gymnastic movements could be learned through mental practice if they were not practiced physically" (p. 60). Throughout the years, mental rehearsal has been referred to in a variety of ways including mental practice, covert practice, symbolic rehearsal, imagery practice, hypnosis rehearsal, implicit practice, and more recently, visuo-motor behavior rehearsal.

Traditionally, mental rehearsal has been employed to assist in the effective acquisition and retention of a skill and in improved performance of that skill (Richardson, 1967). The effectiveness of mental rehearsal is based upon two physiological facts. First, the classic studies of Jacobson (1932) and Shaw (1940), which were later refined and expanded by Maltz (1969) and Bry (1978), showed that the basal parts of the brain and the central nervous system *could not differentiate* between something that was actually happening versus that which was being vividly visualized. The higher parts of the brain make this differentiation. Second, these studies also showed that when one is vividly visualizing a movement, all those nerves that fire the muscles used in the movement are being electrically stimulated at a lower, yet significant magnitude.

So when I am mentally rehearsing (e.g., riding a bicycle), my body believes that this is actually happening. It then fires all those nerves used to stimulate the muscles in effective bicycling; hence, my body gains experience in bicycling well. Morehouse and Gross (1977) summarized this notion in this way: "It's the imagined result that focuses your body, literally organizing its fibers into carrying out your vision" (p. 109). Mental rehearsal, then, seems to be an efficient and effective adjunct in maximizing both learning and performing.

Using Mental Rehearsal

Absurd? Implausible? Metaphysical? Unbelievable? All sorts of people who have to perform and produce in pressurized situations are discovering the values of mental rehearsal. For many of them, whether they are in sports, the performing arts, or in business, mental rehearsal is the essential component that helps them organize, prepare, and channel their efforts.

In sports. You may have witnessed ski racers mentally rehearsing their upcoming runs by waggling their hand as if it were going through the gates. In these instances they *are* their hands in which they visualize themselves going down the course. A top ski racer like Phil Mahre says he might mentally rehearse skiing the course as many as 30 times before the actual run. During these mental rehearsals he will visualize what line he wishes to take through each gate and how he wants to be set up for the next gate. He will also visualize the desired flowing rhythm of his skiing as well as finishing with a positive result.

I have always marveled at how high jumper Dwight Stones can stand at the start of the runway, mentally rehearsing each step and movement of his jump. He stands there almost interminably rehearsing his jump, and then, all of a sudden, he glides down the approach and executes the jump (in most cases) just as he had visualized it.

Jack Nicklaus (1974) has described how he mentally rehearses each shot he takes, even on the practice tee. He visualizes how it feels going through the whole swing, hitting the ball cleanly, observing its flight, and seeing it gently landing in its desired location.

An increasing number of top bodybuilders are using mental rehearsal to literally program their workouts. Tom Platz, for instance, visualizes which muscle group he plans to exercise well in advance of arriving at the gym. He mentally rehearses the specific exercises, how he wants them to feel, and envisions those muscles becoming huge and ripped.

Even though mental rehearsal is more frequently used in static state efforts where the performers have breaks in the action (e.g., between golf shots or gymnastic rotations), it can also be employed in such continuous action events as football, baseball, and soccer. In these sports athletes can mentally rehearse their performance goals and states before the event. Once the event is under way, all they have to do is match their actions with these programmed states. They also can facilitate this by becoming their optimal performance animal. Finally, at time-outs or breaks in the action they can re-create their desired performance states so that they keep in touch with what they need to do.

In the performing arts. An increasing amount of various performing artists are learning how to mentally rehearse. Traditionally, it was believed that all performers had to do was physically rehearse their programs and everything would be okay. Today, many are including mental rehearsal as an adjunct to their physical rehearsals.

Various types of dancers are learning how to relax and center during their stretching. From this base they mentally rehearse all the moves and sequences in their routines. They also visualize themselves on opening night—complete with costumes, lights, and an audience—skillfully and gracefully dancing. They make these mind movies as vivid, detailed, and realistic as possible and repeatedly rehearse them.

Actors and actresses also use mental rehearsal, not so much to help them remember their lines, but to help them become the characters they wish to portray. Being their characters, they visualize how they would move, gesture, talk, and project themselves. More than any other performers, actors use mental rehearsal to program and immerse themselves into becoming their images.

Soloist musicians also greatly rely on mental rehearsal. Like actors, these musicians do not use mental rehearsal to remember the notes and sequences; rather, they employ mental rehearsal to help them in creating the atmosphere, mood, and feeling of the piece they are going to play.

Even pageant contestants have found great success with mental rehearsal. They know that they only have one chance to perform well. For months in advance, these contestants mentally rehearse being in Atlantic City, for example, presenting themselves in a poised and confident manner. They know that by mentally rehearsing all the aspects of their performances, their bodies will believe that they are actually in Atlantic City and will gain precious experience in performing well. Then when they actually arrive, they will believe they have an edge over the other contestants, for many parts of their minds and bodies have already gone through the pageant!

In business. A greater variety of business people are starting to see the benefits of using mental rehearsal in their daily jobs. Traditionally, speakers and trainers, being the performing artists in business, have relied on mental rehearsal. They have used mental rehearsal to practice making presentations so that their messages are informative and applicable.

Within recent years, more salespeople have been regularly using mental rehearsal to organize and to integrate their sales presentations. They have found mental rehearsal not only to be very helpful in the presentations themselves, but also in enabling them to be more aware and responsive to their prospects. Hence, not only can they better present the benefits of their products, they can also better design more appropriate services to meet the prospect's needs and goals.

Even managers and executives are starting to use mental rehearsal. Many have found success in employing mental rehearsal before meetings, interviews, presentations, evaluations, and planning sessions. They have discovered that by taking the time to relax and mentally rehearse what they want to do and be, they are both more effective and efficient in their efforts. Some even regularly set aside time before or at the beginning of a meeting to have all the participants mentally rehearse what each wants to accomplish!

Mental rehearsal is evolving to be an essential ingredient for any effective performance. Its applications are expanding as its effectiveness becomes more widely known. It is now being employed by people ranging from traditional athletes to nontraditional entrepreneurs. I even know of comedians, competitive rock drillers, and tournament poker players who regularly use mental rehearsal to program themselves and to stay focused on what they need to do. In an increasing number of circles, mental rehearsal is starting to become as indispensable to good performance as proper equipment or good coaching. It is that important.

The Mental Imagery Program

Now that you have a pretty good idea of the processes of imaging, let's spend a little time organizing these processes into an orderly sequence. Because it incorporates all the essential ingredients, let's use mental rehearsal to illustrate how to use mental imagery in performance. Again, if you are not a visual imager, translate this sequence into your own imagery sense.

Setting the Stage

With any use of imagery you must start from a base of relaxation. Employ your unique style of relaxing to arrive at a pleasant state of ease. Remember, much of the effectiveness of the vividness of your images is dependent on your being deeply relaxed.

Once you are relaxed, create the scene you wish to rehearse. Use all your mental sense to vividly create your scene in as much detail as possible. What is in your scene? What are the colors and textures of the objects? What can you smell and what can you feel? What sounds do you hear? Create such a precise picture that a photograph of your scene could not even compare with your conception.

After you have created your scene, place yourself in it. *Be* in that scene and *feel* yourself moving in your scene. You are no longer a passive observer viewing a mental movie. You are now the actor or actress in that movie. Now play out the sequence of steps and movements in that scene that leads you to your desired goals. Be very specific in experiencing all the minute details of your actions. Control all the sequences in the scene. Achieve a sense that you are in control of everything. You are now not only the actor or actress in your mind movie, but the producer and director as well!

It is not only essential to feel the processes of the action, but also the desired outcomes. Focus on how it feels at the end of the shot, movement, presentation, stroke, or event. Feel the release of the basketball and see it swish through the hoop. Feel the click of the golf ball and see it flying down the middle of the fairway. Feel the toe-off and see yourself bounding forward. Really structure your scenario so you have an idea of what you want to achieve and so that you achieve it.

For example, when I am bowling in league play and I am sitting awaiting my turn, I am visualizing the lane in great detail, ranging from the grain to the oil to the pins. In this picture I then mentally rehearse my delivery. I go into this scene and feel the proper footwork, swing, release, and follow-through. I am so precise in my visualizing that I can feel the tips of my fingers in the ball and my left foot stopping 2 inches from the foul line. I next visualize the ball powerfully rolling down the alley on the exact line I want. I then see it break sharply toward the pocket 12 feet from the pins. I always end this mental rehearsal with the ball churning through the pins, driving each one into the pit. And then I go up and actually do it!

It is important that you visualize both the process or the steps in your action as well as the desired results. You are then programming your body-mind and will be able to revise your mental rehearsals in order to make them even more appropriate and effective.

The Components of Mental Rehearsal

The applications of mental rehearsal can be divided into two major components: programming and revising. Both components need to be utilized in order to obtain the best overall results from this form of visualizing.

Programming.   This process may range in time from mentally rehearsing your efforts in the Olympics 3 years from now to visualizing how you are going to hit a 9-iron shot 3 seconds from now. McCluggage (1977) called this latter form of programming "mental preplay" in which the performer preplays the swing, the flight of the ball, and the desired result almost as if the process imprints itself on some kind of mental videotape.

Taking this analogy one step further, this mental videotape machine programs images of the action into the great biocomputer called the human being. The body-mind then has a clear blueprint of the desired processes and can go about visualizing them. Mental programming provides direction, models, and parameters for the desired action.

For example, if I were cross-country skiing, I might visualize myself smelling the cool crisp air, seeing my breath, and hearing the wind blowing through the snow-covered pines. I would then feel myself in that scene and visualize how the rhythm of my poling feels, how my hips and knees move, how I toe-off, and how my skis effortlessly glide over the fluffy snow. I would also visualize how well I go up and down hills and how smoothly I make turns. If I were in a race, I would complete my mental rehearsal by seeing and feeling myself passing people, feeling fresh and strong, crossing under the finish banner, hearing the applause from the crowd, and feeling wonderful about myself and my performance!

The more vividly I mentally rehearse, the more effective I become in communicating with and programming the muscles used in that action. The whole rehearsal may take about 10 seconds. So when I am actually in that situation, I can set about performing that action. It is important to trust yourself and allow yourself to execute the action. Don't fall into the trap of trying to think and do at the same time. Remember, your body knows what to do from past experience and from your mental programming. So just put your mind on "automatic pilot" and do it.

As specifically as you visualize, your mental rehearsals will not always be realized. A typical reason for this is that you did not visualize vividly enough. Your body needs very strong, clear, and concise signals in order to get the message from your mind. In the cases when your mental rehearsals were inaccurate or inappropriate, you can apply another form of mental rehearsal to correct them.

Revising. The other component of mental rehearsal is revising the programming of the action. Revising is most effective when it is combined with actual experience from the event. Revising literally means "re-visioning" the whole mental program and making any alterations or corrections in it based on the experience. Revising takes the forms of what McCluggage (1977) called "mental replay" and "recutting your movie."

Let's return to our analogy of the mental videotape machine. After a practice or a performance, the individual replays the whole event on the mind's movie screen and compares what actually happened with what was visualized. After discovering any mistakes or discrepancies in the programming, the performer then visualizes cutting out all those mistake frames and splicing in the correct versions. Hence, the mental programming is now more accurate and appropriate for that event.

Here is how I apply both components of mental rehearsal. At home or in the locker room before a practice, I relax and mentally rehearse how I want to feel and move during my workout. I repeat this mental rehearsal until it becomes second nature to me. For instance, if I am a swimmer, I visualize myself slicing effortlessly through the water. Furthermore, I visualize my arms and shoulders pulling in efficient, rhythmic, and powerful motions. To enhance the effectiveness of these visualizations, I try to feel these motions with as much detail as possible.

Once in the practice session, I stop at various times, close my eyes, and compare what I am actually doing in my mental rehearsals. If there are any discrepancies, I can usually feel the differences. I then re-rehearse the desired motions, repeat them, go back to the practice, and make the necessary physical adjustments. Finally, after the workout, when I am warming down or in the shower, I mentally replay the whole training session, reinforcing those aspects I did well and searching for any mistakes in my mental programming. If I find any mistakes, I visualize cutting them out and splicing in new versions. I then preplay this new version a couple of times to become familiarized with this programming. In this way I am "re-membering" the whole training session.

If I were a salesperson, I might mentally rehearse not only the content of my sales presentation, but also the image I genuinely wanted to project. During breaks or distractions in the sales call (e.g., the phone ringing) I can check how I am performing compared to my rehearsed image. *If* there were discrepancies, I could seek to alter what I am doing to correspond to my mental program. Then after the sales call, I would replay the whole session, searching for mistakes and reinforcing strengths. When I discover errors, I would splice in the proper approaches and practice these during the week. In these ways, I am then using mental rehearsal as a tool to reinforce as well as to improve successful sales techniques.

Jumping In

Mental rehearsal does work, but you must give it your time, energy, and commitment. In the beginning do not worry if you are imaging correctly. Just jump in and start visualizing. As you become more familiar with the process, you can start detailing your pictures more and controlling the actions better.

No matter what kind of mental imagery you use, it is important to repeat the scenarios often. Sometimes, it takes awhile for your mind and body to assimilate the mental programming. As you repeat it, you will not only become more precise with your images, but your mind and body will better understand the message as well.

Any kind of mental imagery is used best with the actual physical action. By using both dimensions in such complementary ways, each serves as a catalyst in more fully maximizing the other.

Thomas Edison once said, "To invent, you need imagination and a lot of junk." Extending this notion to improving your performances in order to invent the kind of performer you would like to be, all you need is to apply your imagination more to the "junk" of your potential so that you can become the jewels of your actualizations.

Applying mental imagery to performing is becoming more widespread, sophisticated, and accepted. Yet mental imagery still retains those unique joys and wonders only our minds can provide. Trust and enjoy your visualizations, and let these movies of the mind be your rehearsals for the you you would like to be!

Chapter 10 Performance Skills

This chapter presented the scope of disassociating and associating mental imagery and how they can be applied in better preparing for performances. Remember the following steps in using any form of mental imagery:

- Start from a base of relaxation. Use your own unique style to relax the body and center the mind.

- Create your mental picture in as much detail as possible. Use all your mental sense in attaining as precise of a description of your scene as you can.

- Put yourself in the scene. Really feel yourself being in your mind movie.

- Control the action of the scenario. Emphasize both the specific steps of the activity as well as achievement of the desired outcomes.

- Repeat the mental imagery often. If possible, combine it with the actual behavior in order to reinforce and refine your mental programming.

- Enjoy and use it! The results will bear out your efforts.

- Notes: _____

    _____

    _____

    _____

    _____

    _____

- Additions or changes to your personal performance formula:

  _____

  _____

  _____

  _____

  _____

chapter 11

Self-Talk

The most important things ever said to us are said by our inner selves.
—Adelaide Bry

Images and words function hand in hand in the brain. We have seen how imagery can be applied to improving performance. A well-rounded utilization of the mind would be incomplete without reviewing how our subverbalizations affect our performances.

We are at least as verbal as we are visual. During our childhoods we were probably much more visual. Dreams, daydreams, and fantasies were commonly present in our daily lives. As we matured and developed, concepts, words, and phrases grew in importance and usage. As we relied more on words to interact with our worlds, our images took more of a back seat. Our words being so important in our everyday lives implies that our words must also be important in our performance lives.

Self-Statements

How we say our words is as important as what we say. What many of us forget is that our words not only communicate our meaning and feeling, but also have a powerful impact on our self-images and, thus, on our performances. Self-statements are those words and phrases I say to myself about myself and about the situations in which I am involved. These subverbalizations influence my views about myself and my situations. The forms and uses of our self-statements can have profound effects on our performance levels.

Think back to your childhood. At one time or another, most of us approached a test in school with the attitude that "There is no way in the world that I am going to pass this test." And it came as little surprise to us when we didn't! On the sandlots if I kept saying to myself, "I hope I don't drop the ball" or "I hope I don't strike out," I usually did! Or during a class presentation if I nervously said to myself, "I hope I don't stutter or forget what I want to say," I usually became a babbling idiot!

Now think back to some of your performances during adolescence. During our first social dances, the more we focused on not stepping on our partner's toes, the more bruises they got! In our early plays or recitals, the more we feared forgetting our lines or steps, the more we did just that. Or the more we begged, "I hope I don't freeze or choke," the more our minds turned to mush! Although most of us were unaware of them back then, our self-statements played a significant role in shaping our performances.

For better or worse, our self-statements are crucial in molding our attitudes and beliefs, reaffirming self-imposed limitations, or breaking ground into new performance frontiers. Self-statements are the most conscious active mental processes that reflect those essential choices to either build ourselves up or drag ourselves down.

Self-statements are the mechanisms that support the principle of the self-fulfilling prophecy. Sure, I may not be able to jump over a tall building in a single bound—yet! But if I constantly say to myself that there is no way in the world that I can ever reach the top of that building, I will never find the stairway.

Self-statements are like a valve that can either shut off or open up the flow of one's performance energies. Properly understood and applied, self-statements can become powerful tools in higher level performances. In order to obtain a better understanding of self-statements, let's start with exploring their basic negative and counterproductive forms.

Types of Negative Self-Statements

Negative forms of self-statements may range from such subtleties as worrying or continually becoming distracted to such extremes as having anxiety attacks or even to abject terror. All of these negative self-statements set the stage (complete with trap doors and falling sandbags!) for poor performances.

Excessive worrying about how you are going to perform probably constitutes the largest single category of negative self-statements. The following are some common examples of such performances worries:

- I should have prepared better.
- What if my partner doesn't show up?
- I should have been more serious during my practices.
- My coach hates me.
- I just can't seem to organize my thoughts today.
- I never made that shot (or move) before in practice, so there is no way I'll be able to do it now.
- I'm afraid that I am going to make a fool out of myself.
- My mind has gone blank.
- I'm giving up.

Sound familiar? What other similar put-downs did these phrases stir up in your mind?

Related to this first category is the type of self-statement that reflects worry about the possible negative consequences of an upcoming performance. Some typical forms of worrying about possible negative consequences are reflected in the following statement: If I do poorly in this performance, I will . . .

- lose my starting position.
- disappoint my parents.
- never get another opportunity like this again.
- be sent down to the minor leagues.
- be ridiculed by my friends.
- be fired.
- quit.

Again, the more I limit my thinking only toward the potential disasters or toward how I will react when they occur, the less I am able to concentrate effectively, and the more I actually ensure that these disasters will occur.

Negative self-statements can also take the form of being physical distractors, creating oversensitized reactions to the performance situation. "I'm so nervous that my stomach is doing double back flips," "My hands are shaking so badly that I will never be able to play the piano," "My butterflies are turning into hawks," "I'm so fidgety that I just can't relax," and "I feel sick" are some physiological negative self-statements. When I am overly sensitized to my body, I usually end up focusing all my energies on those feelings instead of on the performance tasks I need to accomplish. Take a moment now and think about what parts of your body are most susceptible to the pressures and what you tell yourself about them.

Negative self-statements are frequently devious. Often they play the subtle yet destructive role of distracting the performer. Examples of distractive self-statements include:

- Look at that good looking man (woman) up there in the second row.
- That baby's crying is really starting to get on my nerves.
- I wish I had more time to complete this.
- My teammates are always goofing around.
- I remember back when I was in a similar situation to this.
- That sequence wasn't supposed to be in here.
- Those lights are so bright.

We all become distracted at times. The important thing is what we do after we have become distracted. Mediocre performers seem to be more sensitive to distractions and, in some cases, even create their own distractions. Once distracted, these performers let their minds wander and drift farther away from their optimal performance courses.

Wondering how teammates, colleagues, or even competitors are doing during your performance is another subtle form of negative self-statements. The following are some common examples:

- What does she have that I don't?
- How is my practice partner doing over there on the adjacent court?

- Wow, Joan is already done with the examination.
- How can he do better if we prepared in the exact same way?
- Everybody except me seems to be breezing through this section.
- My potential next opponent over there looks really sharp.
- The rest of the class seems to be much brighter than I.

Continually wondering about how others are doing while you are performing opens up the floodgates to other distractions and put-downs.

One final category of negative self-statements is reflecting on one's overall poor self-image. For example:

- I am terrible at this.
- This is just awful.
- I'll never amount to anything.
- After I fail, I won't be able to face anybody.
- I was a fool to think that I could ever do this.
- If only I were smarter, then I could learn this movement.
- This poor performance will prove to everybody that I am totally incompetent.

These put-downs not only affect our performance efforts, they also infect our overall images of ourselves.

Like an unchecked infection, these types of negative self-statements fester and spread throughout the entire individual. These put-downs serve no other purpose than to reinforce pessimistic attitudes, low self-concepts, and, eventually, resignation.

The Powers of Self-Statements

Much of the power of these negative self-statements lies in the fact that *we have probably been saying these things to ourselves for such a long time that we are unaware that we are saying them at all.* These self-statements become so automatic that whenever we encounter a situation befitting our pessimistic beliefs, we are programmed to put ourselves down as we have been doing for years.

Here is a very common example. How many of you are bad at math? For those of you admitting it, how long have you been telling yourself that garbage? If you took the time to discover the roots of these negative self-statements, they may go all the way back to first grade when you had a bad day and flunked a subtraction test! You then probably started criticizing yourself and eventually began generalizing that you were (and always would be) bad at any kind of math. Hence, believing you were terrible at all math, you gave up striving to improve.

The dangerous thing about this sequence of judging, generalizing, and extrapolating is that your mind—being the trusting entity it is—seeks to confirm any self-statement. So when you are, for example, balancing your checkbook, a little bit of your subconscious is actually setting out to prove that you are still bad at math! When your figures inevitably do not balance, you usually conclude by saying, "See, I'm still awful at this. I don't know why I even try anymore." As a result, these automatic put-downs retain and even strengthen their holds on you.

Judging Yourself

Harshly judging yourself and generalizing your put-downs eats away at your performance energies. At a recent running of the Golden Spike Marathon in Brigham City, Utah, I had quite a struggle, which was amplified by my harsh put-downs of myself. It was one of those days when my rhythm was never free and smooth. Becoming oversensitive to every little pain in my body, I began worrying and letting the little demons in my mind run wild. The little pains soon became unbearable. Although the pains were quite real, worrying about them made them much worse. I started having doubts, frustrations, fears, and began judging myself. These judgments led to the generalization that it was impossible for me to ever run a marathon really well and I became convinced that it was hopeless. By 15 miles I was already rehearsing when and how I would drop out, as well as what I would say to people. At 16 miles I did. Even though I was fit enough to run 36 miles, my put-downs sapped my strength and resolve so that all I could run was less than half of that.

Judging, generalizing, and extrapolating reflect a tryer's mentality. These people usually end up saying things such as, "You dummy. You tried so hard, but couldn't do it." Judging and trying feed each other and invariably lead to more put-downs and fears, stronger limitations, and poorer performances.

What Our Bodies Hear

What few of us realize is that when we say these negative self-statements, many parts of our bodies are actually hearing them. Some of the most dramatic examples of our body-minds hearing our put-downs come from the talk about our health and body images.

Do you remember the late comedienne Totie Fields? She was that short, rotund, funny lady who always used to joke about her weight during her acts, saying things such as, "You know, I've tried so many diets that I've finally decided that the only way I'm ever going to lose any weight is to lose a leg." Funny? Not really. She contracted phlebitis, lost a leg, and eventually died from the complications. Coincidence? Probably—but maybe not.

Most businesses, teams, and organizations have a person who is renowned for his skepticism and cynicism and who always plays the role of the "devil's advocate." My old campus was no different. We had a professor who enjoyed taking the unpopular side of an issue. His favorite line for rejecting a different point of view was, "No, I can't see that, I just can't see that at all." Then one day it dawned on me that of course he couldn't see anything! He wore what seemed to be inch-thick glasses! Coincidence? Probably—but maybe not.

I work with many women performers and athletes who have the eating disorder, bulimarexia. Those inflicted ingest tremendous amounts of food and then, feeling guilty about it, induce vomiting. "I just can't stomach that about myself," is one of their most frequently used put-downs. And they don't. Many of them binge eat and vomit or use laxatives and diuretics as many as six times per day. Coincidence? Probably—but maybe not.

When I mentioned these instances at a recent conference, a woman came up to me at a break and said, "You know, it now all makes sense. I was recently promoted from within the ranks into a management position. I was the first woman to ever attain that level in the corporation. I quickly discovered that I had to relate with my old colleagues differently. Worse yet, my chauvinistic supervisors kept on giving me new roles and assignments. Wanting to do a good job as well as prove that a woman could be successful in such a position, each time I was given a new responsibility I would say to myself, 'I can absorb that' or 'I can take that in.' I now realize that I started taking in everything in my life. I lost the power to say no, especially to food. So, within the last 6 months I have 'absorbed' 40 pounds."

Are all of these merely coincidences? Maybe. But there is increasing evidence showing that our minds and bodies seek to actualize whatever we imprint with our self-statements. To further understand this, take a moment to ask yourself this question, "How much of you has ever heard of you?" My left little finger has never heard of a Kubistant. Neither has my right leg. Only a small portion in the left hemisphere of my brain knows what a Kubistant is. So if I am putting myself down, exaggerating something, employing sarcasm, or using a metaphor, the little part of my brain knows that these are mental devices, but the rest of me is translating these as commands. It then seeks to bring these statements into actuality.

Like fertile ground, the body-mind *does not care* what we implant. It will nurture and grow either weeds or corn. The body-mind trusts that what we implant with our beliefs is in our best interests. Being a very trusting organism, it views these messages as commands and starts taking steps to transform them into reality. We really do become what we think about.

We have seen some of the forms and powers of negative self-statements. If they can have such power in negative forms, *they can also have such power in positive forms.* First, let's get rid of these negative forms.

Transforming Negative Self-Statements

Dr. Jerry Nims, an old colleague of mine, is fond of saying, "What would happen if someone on the street came up to you and told you all that negative stuff you tell yourself? You wouldn't take it from him so why should you take it from you?" Why indeed!

Negative self-statements are energy, and, as such, the goal for any form of counterproductive energy is not to get rid of it, but to redirect it. Merely trying to "think positive" on top of a base of negative put-downs does not work. Performers must learn how to break down their negative self-statements and put them back together in more productive ways.

To begin transforming your negative self-statements into positive ones, you must first become *aware* of those put-downs you have been telling yourself. Remember that much of the power these negative self-statements have over you is that they have become so automatic that you are no longer aware of what you are saying. Therefore, plan at least 1 week for awareness activities. You may want to carry a little notebook around with you to write down all the put-downs you discover. Divert a little of your consciousness so that you continually monitor all of your self-statements.

When you catch yourself putting yourself or others down, worrying excessively, doubting too much, or thinking pessimistically, congratulate yourself! That's right, congratulate yourself. When you discover a put-down, write it in your notebook. Avoid the temptations of judging yourself or putting yourself down further. You may find that you are tempted to say, "Now, isn't that stupid the way I put myself down," "You dummy," or "Don't do that." When you react in these ways, you are perpetuating and deepening the pattern of negative self-statements. Don't judge your put-downs, just write them down.

After you have caught yourself using negative self-statements, stop whatever you are doing or saying, actively challenge that self-statement, and rephrase it with a more positive one. When you phrase the new statement, avoid using such double negatives as "Don't do it that way,"

"Don't forget," or "Don't blow up." Rather, phrase your new statements using the positive terms you want to implement such as, "Do it this way," "Remember your lines," or "Remain patient." In order for you to best change your self-statements, your body and mind need simple, direct, and positive instructions.

As your monitoring week proceeds, I think you will become amazed at how many negative self-statements you discover and at the impact they have had on your beliefs and efforts. As you become more aware, begin extending this process to your performance specialty. Go through the same congratulating and rephrasing so that you can start redirecting your performance beliefs.

An example is in order. I have recently discovered that I am covertly pessimistic about my poker abilities. My usual approach to the game included the following self-statements:

- I wonder how long it will take me to lose tonight.
- Let's see what kind of stupid mistakes I can make in this game.
- I am really dumb at this game.

Now after catching these put-downs, I immediately *rephrase* them as follows:

- Let's see how much I can *win* tonight.
- *If* I make a mistake, I will learn from it.
- I am continually learning more and enjoying this game.

Later on, and especially before a game, I will use and *repeat* the following positive self-statements:

- I am a good poker player.
- I am doing the best job I can.
- I am an aware person.
- I concentrate well.
- I am going to have fun tonight.

Many performers enjoy catching themselves on their put-downs, making a game of it. With this perspective they can become more aware of themselves and place themselves in a better position to transform their negative self-statements into positive ones.

Awareness of all your put-downs does certainly weaken their power over you, and this is the necessary first step in replacing them. The next step is to go through Ellis' (1973) *ABC* process of challenging your negative self-statements. He believes that the consequences (*C*) of any action—such as flat performances, freezing, or choking—is not due to the activating event (*A*) or the performance situation, but to your belief system (*B*) concerning that event or situation. Your belief systems are comprised of all those self-statements—positive and negative—that you tell yourself about yourself or your situation. Upon realization, the next step is to actively dispute (*D*) or challenge your counterproductive self-statements. Either verbally or subverbally, compose sentences that dispute the logic, reason, and validity of your put-downs. For example:

- Yes, I am not prepared well enough, and I will do the best job I can.
- Even if I fail, it won't be the end of the world.
- At least I now know what to work on.
- Yeah, I might not be winning, but I am playing much better.
- Yes, I am not making my quota, but I am getting closer.
- I may have a lousy backhand, *and* I am still a wonderful person.

Each time you hear yourself putting yourself down, immediately stop whatever you are doing and actively dispute or challenge the statement. Only through this process will you eventually break those negative self-statements and formulate new positive ones so that you can attain more productive effects (*E*).

Using this *ABCDE* approach, you will quickly discover how fragile, counterproductive, and even absurd your put-downs really are. Also, by challenging them, you will start assuming more responsibility for your belief systems, and then you will be in a position to create more positive self-statements.

Affirmations

Positive self-statements are called affirmations. Affirmations are not wishing and hoping, nor are they bragging. Rather, they simply consciously affirm or confirm qualities, skills, and attributes that already exist in the individual. High-level performers of all kinds use affirmations in many ways to remind them to reinforce their positive performance abilities. These affirmations help settle as well as organize so that their performance efforts will be more directed and effective.

Each of the three general categories of affirmations—basic, activity-specific, and process—has its own applications and uses. Let's look at each of these more closely.

Basic Affirmations

Basic affirmations are nice, general, and positive self-statements that confirm one's essential choices and good qualities. For example:

- Every day in every way I am better and better.
- I like myself.
- I am the captain of my ship; I am the master of my fate.
- I trust my abilities.
- I am relaxed.
- I forgive my errors.
- Sure I can.
- Can do.
- I enjoy what I do.
- I am on my side.
- I always do the best job I can.
- I am proud of my efforts.
- I can do anything I choose to do.

(Fill in others that apply to you.)

- _____

- _____

- _____

- _____

You may have noticed that some of these basic affirmations are not new. A few of them have been around for scores of years. You can use these basic affirmations almost any time. You may certainly want to use them at the start of your day, in conjunction with your relaxation, and whenever any fears and doubts creep into you. They are nice ways of taking you back to your basic senses of control and well-being.

Activity-Specific Affirmations

This second form of affirmations reminds you of the specific skills and attributes you need for good performances and reinforces them. For example:

- I am a good _____
- I am an efficient _____
- I am a creative _____
- I am a relaxed _____
- I am a courageous _____
- I am a strong _____
- I am a purposeful _____
- I am a graceful _____

(Fill in others that apply to you.)

- I am a _____
- I am a _____
- I am a _____

These activity-specific affirmations are not bragging; they are simply reminders of competence. Use these affirmations immediately before a practice or performance as you are stretching or mentally rehearsing. You can also use them immediately following your practice or performance to enhance the good feelings and senses of accomplishment from your efforts.

Process Affirmations

Process affirmations consist of one or two positive words that you say to yourself during the performance. Process affirmations quiet and focus the mind as well as draw upon additional performance energies. These words serve to remind you of those basic states and feelings you wish to tune into. For example:

Yes	Relax	Easy	Rhythm
Smooth	Flowing	Strong	Soft
Stroft (Strong + Soft)	Floating	Gliding	Through it
Go	Slicing	Form	Nice
Focus	Concentrate	Now	Explode
Bust it	Do it	C'mon	Now
Pump	Stroke	Good	

(Fill in others that apply to you.)

_____ _____ _____ _____

Soft-sounding affirmations (e.g., "Yes" or "Easy") work best earlier in the practice or performance. Forceful-sounding process affirmations (e.g., "Go" or "Bust it") are most effective in the latter parts of the practice or performance. One word can often spark many thoughts and feelings. Use your process affirmations as your performance spark plugs.

Like various forms of mental imagery, all three of these forms of affirmations must be applied. Learn when and where in your performances each is most effective. The beauty of using affirmations is that they not only aid in improving your performances, but they also seep into the rest of your life as well.

Guidelines for Using Affirmations

Affirmations work; however, in order for them to be most effective, it is crucial to construct and phrase them properly. Incorrectly constructed and phrased affirmations lose much of their punch and might even be smokescreens for negative self-statements. It might be helpful to consider some general procedures for constructing powerful affirmations.

First, make sure you have redirected your negative self-statements. Remember, placing affirmations on top of a base of negative self-statements does little good. Continually monitor yourself in order to discover old as well as new put-downs. As you discover them, go through your challenging and replacing processes.

Second, as with mental imagery, begin using affirmations from a nice, relaxed state. Being relaxed will open up the pathways to those attributes and qualities you wish to affirm.

Third, always construct and phrase your affirmations in a positive manner, without using any qualifications. Say, "I am a nimble rock climber" instead of "On every Wednesday sometimes I am a pretty nimble rock climber!" Or, "I am a competent salesperson" instead of "When a buyer is in a good mood, I have a great product, and the stars are in proper alignment then I am a fairly good salesperson!" Qualifications, exceptions, and reservations simply weaken your affirmations and open you up to further put-downs. *Be positive.* Period.

Also, when you are constructing your affirmations, it is important that you avoid using phrases having double negative connotations. It is an interesting phenomenon *that the brain and the central nervous system do not process negative words.* So if I say to myself, "I am *not* clumsy," "I will *not* choke," "I will *not* smoke today," "I will *not* stammer during my presentation," or "I will *not* yell at the kids today," what my brain and central nervous system are really hearing is that "I am———clumsy," "I will———choke," "I will———smoke today," "I will———stammer during my presentation," or "I will———yell at the kids today!"

Those of you who have ever raised children are quite aware that how you phrase a statement can really influence a child's action. If you say, "Susie, don't touch that hot stove," what does Susie do? By phrasing the statement in such a way, what Susie's brain and central nervous system heard was, "Susie, *do* touch that hot stove!" You put the notion of hot stove into her consciousness. It would have been much better to say, "Susie, come here." Phrase your statements to yourself and to others not in terms of what you do not want done (I know, I used a double negative!), but in terms of what you want done.

One of the habits I have carried over from my childhood is the compulsion for kicking stones. Many pairs of shoes have been ruined and too many toes have been stubbed pursuing this passion. Kicking stones led me to discover the necessity of properly phrasing or programming my self-statements. When I would be kicking stones along a sidewalk and someone would approach me from the other direction, I used to say to myself, "Now don't kick it near them." I didn't realize that most of me was hearing, "Now *do* kick it near them!" Inevitably, the stone would fly true to its programmed course, usually hitting the person in the shins or becoming entangled in the spokes of a bicycle! My intentions were good, but my programming was faulty.

Fourth, construct your affirmations in the present tense as much as possible. The only time period over which I have complete control is the present. Phrasing too many of your affirmations in the future tense turns them into wishing, hoping, and expecting. Say, "I am a good swimmer" instead of "I will definitely win seven gold medals in the 1988 Olympics." Or, "I will always win." Or, "I am doing all the things I need to do in order to reach this quarter's quota" instead of "I will exceed this quarter's quota by 17%." In each instance, you have more direct control over the former example than you do over the latter. Remember, you seldom have total control over the outcome, so put your efforts into and phrase your affirmations around that which you can most directly control.

Finally, continually repeat your affirmations and build upon them. Self-statements are like muscles: They are always in a dynamic state of flux. If you do not continually reinforce and strengthen them, they will atrophy, stagnate, and become counterproductive. Remember, if you are not continually building yourself up, you are covertly dragging yourself down.

Most theories of learning agree that it takes about 21 repetitions of something before it is understood and integrated. So repeat your basic, activity-specific, and process affirmations to yourself. As you do, you will discover how enjoyable it is to affirm yourself and your skills.

High-level performances are founded not on what you don't have, but on what you do have. It makes sense, then, that in order to produce your skills and competencies, you have to affirm and remind yourself that you possess them. Properly phrased and used, your self-talk can have a great mobilizing effect on your performance, for you do as you believe.

Chapter 11 Performance Skills

- Self-statements are subverbalizations we say about ourselves and the situations we are in. What we say to and about ourselves, as well as how we say it, has a great deal of influence on our performance levels.

- The basic categories of negative self-statements are (a) worrying about how you are going to perform, (b) worrying about the possible negative consequences of a performance, (c) being overly sensitized to bodily reactions, (d) becoming distracted by wondering how colleagues or competitors are doing, and (e) reflecting on one's poor self-image.

- The power of negative self-statements resides in the fact that we might have been putting ourselves down in the same way for such a long time that we become unaware of what we are doing.

- The first step in changing negative self-statements is to become more aware of how you are putting yourself down, both in your performance activities as well as in the rest of your life.

- After you become more aware of your counterproductive self-statements, construct phrases that actively dispute or challenge them and replace them with positive self-statements of what you want to do or be.

- Positive self-statements (affirmations) remind you of and reinforce what you already are or have.
- The basic categories of positive self-statements in performance are basic affirmations, activity-specific affirmations, and process affirmations. Each has its own roles and functions, so learn to employ each category appropriately.
- The general process for structuring affirmations is to (a) become aware and redirect negative self-statements, (b) start from a state of pleasant relaxation, (c) construct affirmations in a totally positive manner, (d) structure affirmations in the present tense and in ways that emphasize those aspects of your efforts over which you have control, and (e) continually repeat and expand upon your affirmations.
- Notes: _____

  _____

  _____

  _____

  _____

- Additions or changes to your personal performance formula:

  _____

  _____

  _____

  _____

chapter 12

The Dance

There is only the dance.
—T.S. Eliot

The previous chapters have explored high-level performance in a progression from the general mental concepts of attitudes, goals, beliefs, and doing to the more specific applications of relaxation, mental imagery, and self-statements. If anything has become clear, it is that there are a multitude of components, combinations, and intangibles needed to perform well. Not only do these vary from activity to activity, but from situation to situation, phase to phase, and especially from individual to individual.

But what about the actual performance itself? Given all the planning and preparation in the world, there are certain issues and emphases that can only be addressed within the context of the performance. This chapter will explore some of these issues.

Economy of Effort

One thing that stands out in observing almost all high-level performers is the ease with which they accomplish quite complicated and intricate tasks. There is very little wasted energy or movement. They almost seem to float through tough and challenging situations that would make lesser performers stumble. Even in such violent sports as football and boxing, there is a grace and effortlessness in great performers at which the rest of us can only marvel.

Take, for example, the instances of elite athletes performing in very close quarters. Great racquetball, squash, and handball players waste little effort. Beyond that, they almost seem to be engrossed in a kind of dance. Even though they are opponents, the coordination of movements between them is quite beautiful. World class rock climbers and aikido masters almost seem to defy gravity and the laws of physics with their gliding movements. Really good salespeople make their sales presentations and the relationships with their prospects seem so easy and natural that one would think anyone could do it. Top professional speakers interact so smoothly with their audiences that it almost seems that everyone is following some master script.

Even team activities have their dancers. The communication, rhythm, timing, and synchronization between teammates frequently transcends the competitive situation. The passing between hockey or soccer players, the communication between pitcher and catcher, the rhythmic setting of the volleyball, or the timing of the basketball "ali-oop" play would bring applause from even the finest dance troupe.

A mark of high-level performers is to make complicated movements look easy. It is only when novices attempt these movements that they discover all the intricacies involved and then can truly appreciate the experts' mastery.

Clearly, high-level performing is more than brute force. No matter how physical or violent the sport, elite performers can be considered artists. Their execution, poise, expression, creativity, and ease with which they perform is art. These performers are like dancers floating in some kind of higher order ballet. In describing the attributes of superior athletes, Leonard (1975) concluded, "I can't say that a dancer is the Ultimate Athlete. I am quite certain, however, that the Ultimate Athlete is a dancer" (p. 267).

As in any dance, there are the obvious primary dancers and major themes. But there are also supporting dancers and subtle themes that are essential in providing the balance, depth, perspective, and tone to the overall performance. These combinations of the obvious and subtle roles, components, and dynamics are what make this higher order dance both so challenging and so elusive.

Momentum

One of the best examples of the dance in performing is momentum. It is sought after, desired, and even expected, but it often remains elusive, misunderstood, and even mysterious. It has been fondly called Mo, Big M, The Force, The Sixth Player (in basketball), The Twelfth Man (in football), and The Upper Hand. Sportscasters love talking about it and embellish it to the point where it almost seems to become a physical entity.

Momentum is an indirect by-product of optimal performance. It is a sign that the performer has brought together the mind and body and is channeling performance energies efficiently. Momentum is an indication that a performer is in his or her optimal performance zone and has achieved an optimal level of arousal.

Gaining momentum and maintaining momentum are two separate processes. In many ways, gaining momentum is the easier of the two to achieve. Most performers know the things they need to do well in order to succeed and, hence, gain momentum. However, once they have achieved it, they are frequently less sure of what to do in order to maintain it.

Very often, individuals and teams ease off too much after they have gained momentum. They "rest on their laurels," start thinking too much, and forget to continue doing the things that gained them the momentum in the first place. The result is that they drop below their optimal performance zones and start to struggle. On the other hand, once they have gained momentum, some individuals and teams become greedy and want more of it. So they start trying harder, forcing things, and becoming too intense. The result is that they push themselves beyond their optimal performance zones so that everything soon becomes fragmented and foreign.

To maintain momentum, you must balance staying relaxed with concentrating on your essential emphases. Stay in the flow of your performance, but also remain in control of yourself. The worst thing you can do is to believe, "I've got it made now." Concentrate on continuing doing the things well that gained you the momentum in the first place. View momentum as a feedback mechanism that says you are on track. Be pleased that you are "in the flow," but take the proper steps to ensure that you remain there.

Streaks and Slumps

Two interesting extensions of momentum are the extremes of streaks and slumps. Although these are sometimes interpreted as being qualities of the inconsistent or mediocre performer, streaks and slumps are issues that every performer occasionally encounters. Nothing can be as joyful as a streak of high-level performing or as frustrating as a prolonged slump.

Streaks. Streaks are wonderful and seem to make all the previous struggles worthwhile. However, the quickest way to end a streak is to think about it, analyze it, or wonder when it is going to end. Remember, you cannot effectively perform and think at the same time. The best advice for streaks is to keep on doing and continue "playing out of your head."

Just as in peak performances, streaks can be planned and predicted, but just to a degree. Focus on your performance of the essentials. As the performance proceeds, allow more of your skills and emphases to flow together. The best way to do this is to spend a greater proportion of your concentration in awareness. Paying too much attention to individual segments of your efforts tends to disrupt the flow of the streak. Be aware and stay in the mode of pure doing.

Like a surfer, ride the crest of the wave of your streaks. Although you are on a streak, you must still make decisions and adjustments; it is far from a mindless process. As a surfer must make decisions and adjustments to stay in the critical section of the wave, so must you continue to make decisions and adjustments to stay in your streak. Because you are in the flow of your performance wave, make the cuts and maneuvers so you can maximize your ride.

If you choose to later reflect back on a streak in order to learn from it, you may wish to consider several factors. Remember the feelings, sensations, thoughts, attitudes, and images you experienced during the streak; then write them down. See if there are any common patterns of these throughout your streaks. For example, many performers often experience gliding and floating feelings, sensations of peace and calm, or the courage and trust to just "go for it." If you discover any such patterns, focus on them, for they are often the instigators that can trigger new streaks.

Some performers are prone to streaks while others are not. In many respects, nothing is better than a nice, boring, high-level performance. This shows a high integration of abilities and a consistent application of skills. However, those performers who have streaks, learn from them, and are able to elevate their overall performance levels based on those lessons are the ones who tend to carve out performance frontiers for the rest of us. So enjoy your streaks, learn from them, and see how far you can ride them in improving your overall levels of performance.

Slumps. Slumps are quite a different matter. In the midst of a slump is always the temptation to pick apart your whole performance style. While some parts may need to be reviewed, on the whole, too much worry and analysis simply prolong the slump. Slumps are real tests of your positive mental attitudes and belief systems. It is easy to be positive when things are going well. Slumps provide you with a challenge to be positive when things are rough.

During these times redirect your energies and priorities. Focus on what you can control and still do well. Emphasize passing instead of shooting, fielding instead of hitting, or supporting instead of leading. When they are in slumps, mediocre performers tend to generalize that they are doing everything poorly. However, slumps, in a crazy way, are really opportunities for you to learn to broaden your skills and understanding of both your activity and your performance style.

These are also times to review the basic aspects and qualities that originally made you perform well. Too often we overemphasize the subtle nuances that might contribute 1% to our performances while neglecting the basic element that contributes the other 99%. Review these basic skills, emphases, and attitudes you had when you were performing well, and simply start doing them again.

It is a myth that you have to have a clear and total understanding of why something went wrong in order to correct it. Quite often, even if you do totally discover why something went wrong (which is unlikely), it will not necessarily put you in a position to perform better. After all, you don't have to be a master mechanic to drive well. Rather, slumps are good times to reassess your goals. Often, you will find that goals that were appropriate as little as 3 months ago, no longer are. The more you try to stick with those outdated goals, the more prolonged your slumps will be.

Sometimes you will discover that you are putting too much pressure on yourself to win or be successful. Retain your goals to win or be successful, but keep in sight all your subgoals of the little things you need to do to perform well. Remember, there are many little steps on the road to success.

One curious factor I have found common to many performers experiencing slumps is that they do not prepare well. They may think they are preparing, but what they are really doing is worrying, overanalyzing, and covertly putting themselves down. Spend your time and energy physically and mentally preparing for your performances. Turn down your emotions and judgments and simply focus on the things you need to do. Although it is good to analyze, it is important to start doing again. Get back to a pure mode of doing while practicing or performing. Start trusting and believing in yourself again and just go out and do.

Quite often, slumps are caused or exacerbated by imbalances in the rest of the performer's life such as relationship problems, chemical abuse, and counterproductive personal habits. Neglecting or avoiding some areas of their lives, or simply needing a rest may also make it very difficult for a person to perform consistently well. Some time away from the performance specialty may be necessary before the performer can do anything about the slump.

Keeping a sense of humor and demonstrating control are both invaluable during a slump. A sense of humor gives perspective and helps you get back in touch with your positive mental attitudes. Remember that humor promotes, whereas worry prolongs. The key word, however, in handling slumps is *control*. Control those elements you can influence or still do well. Trust that you will come out of your slump. Until then, focus and continue to build upon those things you can control.

Errors

Errors are probably the single greatest emphasis for improvement in the performance dance. With errors there is little chance that the performance will flow easily, much less be successful. However, in any performance situation, there are many more possibilities for errors than there are for proper execution. Performers must first learn about their errors in order to minimize and eventually eliminate them.

Just as in most other areas of high-level performance, there are usually commonalities or patterns in the types of errors a person makes. Spend a moment now and list the patterns of your performance errors.

_____   _____   _____

_____   _____   _____

_____   _____   _____

_____   _____   _____

If you search long enough, you will find definite patterns to your performance errors. These patterns may not initially be obvious to you, but discovering them is an important key to performance success.

Preparation. Poor preparation is the hallmark of the mediocre performer. One of the factors that makes good performances seem so effortless is that the performer has meticulously prepared for that effort. Even in familiar performance situations, good performers understand that they can take nothing for granted; they must prepare.

Many errors occur when the individual is caught by surprise in the performance situation. Incomplete or faulty preparation leaves gaps in the person's abilities to react and to adjust. Poor decisions, wasted time and energy, disjointed efforts, and disappointing performances usually result.

High-level performers from all kinds of endeavors take pride in their comprehensive preparation, both physical and psychological. Many top executives prepare extensively for each of their meetings, even if those meetings are with only one person. Most professional speakers abide by the general formula of preparing 4 hours for the first hour of a speech and 2 hours for every hour after that. Consistently effective salespeople prepare so well for their prospects that they will be able to handle any question or contingency that arises. All of these professionals view preparation not as time wasted, but as time invested. Many believe that after so much preparation the easy part is the actual performance!

An interesting trend is now occurring whereby elite physical performers (athletes and performing artists) are giving more emphasis to mental preparation, while elite mental performers (business people, artists, and musicians) are giving more emphasis to physical preparation. The physical performers are employing formal relaxation, mental rehearsal, role playing, and affirmations, while the mental performers are participating in swimming, running, and aerobics. Both camps are seeing the benefits of a well-rounded base of preparation.

Preparation is not only a core ingredient for the minimizing of errors, it is also essential for consistently effective performances. "Be prepared" is not only the motto of the Boy Scouts, but for many elite performers as well.

Tightness. Being too tight takes the forms of trying too hard, worrying, becoming angry, anticipating and expecting too much, putting too much pressure on self, and succumbing to fear. The stresses of the performance situation combined with the individual's anxieties frequently dull and constrict skills and abilities. Where performers may erroneously conclude that they were not "up" enough, it is probably more a matter of them being "too up."

All performers have to learn to control, to cope, and to channel their emotions, especially anger. Anger is a common result of being too tight; it stems from frustrations, fears, and doubts that get out of hand. It is a very, very rare individual who can productively use anger. For must of us anger has deleterious effects. Like the quick energy gain from a candy bar, anger may temporarily raise performance levels, but it will soon drag the efforts down to a lower level.

Errors of tightness frequently revolve around spending too little time in the present. One expects and anticipates what might happen in the future or reminisces and frets about what happened in the past. The key to bringing us back to the present is our old friend relaxation. Remember, it is very difficult to be tight or out of the present when you are relaxing. When you don't know what else to do, relax. It is home base.

Looseness.   At the other extreme are the errors of being too loose. Mental lapses, loose strokes, and missing many easy opportunities are common examples of errors of looseness. One thing coaches or managers fear in their teams is complacency. They know that the more complacent their teams are, the more susceptible they are to losing their competitive edges and committing errors of looseness. Being nonchalant, overconfident, whimsical, capricious, and lackadaisical are some other precursors to committing errors of looseness.

Being too loose is not the same thing as being too relaxed. Quite often performers who make these kinds of errors are just as conscientious and concerned about their errors as anyone else. The problem lies in the fact that they have difficulty sustaining their intensity. So when others choke or freeze, these performers become too loose and have mental lapses.

On the whole, errors of looseness are easier to prevent and to correct than errors of tightness. The key to correcting them is to use the already existing base of relaxation to help the performer learn how to focus better. Too often these errors evolve from being too aware and not paying enough attention to the details at hand. The individuals must learn how to intensify, attend to, and sustain their efforts without falling into the trap of trying harder. The image of the magnifying glass discussed in chapter 8 is often helpful in conveying the distinction between intensity and trying harder.

Reviewing performance goals and priorities is also helpful in developing the kind of sustained concentration needed to prevent lapses. Hence, proceeding from a base of relaxation, performers can learn how to intensify and sustain their concentrations so that they arrive at a better position to prevent and correct errors of looseness.

We are all human and some errors are inevitable, but what we do with the errors is really the important issue in determining how well we will perform. A nonjudgmental, trusting, and openness to learning attitude is essential in minimizing future performance errors. Many performances are frequently decided by those who make the least number of errors. Learning from past mistakes and discovering patterns of errors provide the base for minimizing them in the future.

After you have learned the patterns of your performance errors and have learned how to minimize them, one of the most important (and difficult) things you must learn is how to be focused without being too tight and how to be relaxed without being too loose. All of this revolves around the ability to concentrate. Focus on your performance goals, prepare physically and mentally, relax, and plunge into your performances. When you do, most errors will be averted, and when you do make an error, you will be in a stronger position to rectify it quickly.

Performance Intangibles

Many elements in performance are difficult to define objectively. These elements are often vague and nebulous, but they do play important roles in effective performance. The following discussion of some of the most prevalent intangibles is meant to be a catalyst from which you can develop a better understanding of what these factors mean in your own performances.

Confidence

Confidence is another one of those overused, abused, and misunderstood notions in performance. I am always amused to hear athletes who haven't won in the last 17 or so outings say, "I feel really confident today!" How can they be?

The notion of confidence seems to be a dumping ground for wishes, hopes, and delusions. It also seems to be a favorite replacement word for a misdirected and swaggering brand of cockiness. When I interview performers in depth who brag that they are confident, I usually find that they are really cocky. This cockiness is usually a smokescreen that masks deficiencies, doubts, fears, and a lack of belief in self.

Confidence is a word I rarely use. Instead, I break it down into its specific components, which are more concrete and manageable. What are the components of your notions of confidence? Take a couple of minutes and list all those factors that contribute to your feeling of confidence. Take the time to list your components. It will be well worth it.

_____   _____   _____

_____   _____   _____

_____   _____   _____

_____   _____   _____

You may have been surprised to discover that your list included factors that you might not have immediately equated with confidence. Things like the home court advantage and familiar surroundings, support from family and friends, good weather, age, a good night's sleep, knowing the weaknesses of your opponent, and feeling strong all have subtle yet important roles in building up your confidence. You might have also been surprised to discover that your list probably did not include many of the more brazen emotions you thought must be related to confidence. Feelings such as being poised, relaxed, calm, assured, controlled, cool, and eager are more prevalent on lists of confidence than the feelings of being cocky, psyched, animalistic, or even aggressive.

Some common factors appear on many lists of confidence. These factors include previous successful experiences, realistic optimism, purpose and goals, quality training, proper mental preparation, trust in skills and abilities, a relaxed alertness, and a continuous honest view of self. These factors are the building blocks of confidence.

Related to confidence is the concept of mental toughness. Mental toughness implies minimizing errors and distractions while maximizing essentials, experience, and execution. It is a feeling that you are "locked into" your tasks at hand. The best representation I have seen for mental toughness is found in Figure 12.1. If I had to replace confidence with any other concept, it would be with mental toughness.

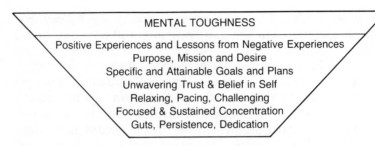

Figure 12.1 Components of mental toughness.

Movement Intangibles

A whole group of performance variables can best be classified as movement intangibles. These include such notions as rhythm, pace, flow, and tempo. Even with performers in the same activity, these movement intangibles can take on quite different meanings.

These notions may very well be the pinnacle of the integration and synthesis in performing. If high-level performance was just a matter of cementing together a variety of disjointed skills, any machine could do it. On the contrary, one of the hallmarks of peak performances is the almost magical integration, outpouring, and flowing between skills, sequences, and phases.

Quite often we try too hard to attain good rhythm, pace, and tempo. As we learn the jargons of our specific activities, we frequently isolate these movement intangibles. "My rhythm is way off today," "I really need to focus on my pacing during this stage," "There seems to be a block in my energy flow," and "My swing tempo doesn't feel right" are examples of these misguided quests. Isolating and overanalyzing these movement intangibles only stifles their emergence.

It should come as no surprise that in most cases the effective zones of these movement intangibles are much slower than what we think. Forcing does little good. It is often much easier to start off slowly and make adjustments upward than it is to start off quickly and try to make adjustments downward.

Striving to gain an understanding of these movement intangibles is one of those instances in which we become too smart for our own good. Leave well enough alone.

Rhythm, pace, flow, and tempo will emerge if you let them be and give them a chance. Take it slowly and allow the natural wisdom of your experiences plus the integration of your mind and body to take over.

Chance Intangibles

Chance intangibles are a group of intangibles that really have nothing to do with performing directly, but have a great deal of influence on the minds of the performers. These intangibles are most often divided into the categories of luck and superstition.

Luck. Luck is something that is neither planned nor under the direct control of the individual, but it frequently affects subsequent performance levels. Good luck can often spur the performer on to greater efforts. "Getting the breaks," "God is on my side today," or "This must be my day" can serve as a kind of placebo that elevates performances.

While good luck is often dismissed, bad luck is much harder to forget. When faced with numerous unlucky experiences, performers can become so distracted worrying about their bad luck that they do not concentrate properly on their efforts. This pattern may become a self-fulfilling prophecy where the performers start generalizing that they are "jinxed" or "predestined" to have bad luck. In these instances the performers allow an intangible or fluke to control them by actually constructing limitations they may never surmount.

Increasingly, more coaches, teachers, and performers are addressing the issue of luck. They are learning how to shrug off (both physically and symbolically) bad luck and go on with their efforts. They have also been recently extrapolating the old Chinese view of good luck that "Chance favors the prepared" to "Luck is where preparation and opportunity meet." They are integrating good luck with preparation and, thus, feel a greater sense of control over it. "I make my own breaks," "I don't deserve it, but I will take it," and "I've earned it" are all examples of the current views of luck being an unplanned but welcome ally.

Superstition.   Superstition is the other major category of the chance intangibles that can have profound effects on the minds and attitudes of performers. The power of superstition lies in the fact that individual performers have generalized isolated occurrences from various situations to the extent that they view them as necessary in all future endeavors.

Singer (1975) summarized superstitions in this way: "Superstitious behaviors can be extremely powerful (like any placebo) in raising performance, especially in the gullible and susceptible" (p. 81).Superstitions can entwine themselves into the performer's attitudes and preparations so that they become integral components of any kind of performance belief or plan. Whether this is right or wrong is not the point. The point is that superstition, like luck, is a reality. The performer's challenge is to minimize the counterproductive superstitions and to maximize the productive ones.

Superstitious behavior falls into two general categories: preparation and process superstitions. As their names imply, preparation superstitions are rituals enacted prior to performance, and process superstitions are rituals followed during the performance. Preparation superstitions may take the form of specific eating and dressing rituals, wearing the same clothes as in the previous successful performance, and various warm-up sequences, among others. Process superstitions may take the form of entering or leaving the court or field in the same prescribed manner, not stepping on lines, knocking on wood, ritual gestures or movements, and scores of others, most of which are only known to the individual. The antics of baseball pitchers are the epitome of superstitious behaviors. Just watch all the mannerisms, quirks, and rituals a pitcher will go through before he throws the ball!

I am not promoting the uses of luck or superstition. What I am saying is that they can be a—but by no means the only—catalyst to increased levels of belief, relaxation, and concentration. If you are a performer who believes in luck or superstition, fine. Use them, avoid generalizing and depending upon them, but let them serve you. Use them as a means—not as an end—to improving your performance levels.

Issues During the Performance

Let's now look at some of the major issues that occur during the actual performance. Naturally, there are some issues that are so unique or rare that they can only be addressed as they occur, but there are some common issues that can be reviewed outside of the situations in which they occur.

As intimated throughout this chapter, each performance and performance situation is unique. High-level performers have learned to accept and even appreciate these unique situations. As many times as I have hit a 3-foot putt, each one—even if I cannot consciously detect it—is unique. The same goes for every plié, scale, speech, employee evaluation, and so on. The performer who expects all circumstances to be identical to previous ones is not going to be able to make the necessary adjustments as variances occur.

The uniqueness of each performing situation implies that we must always adapt and adjust. We have to take our personal formulas into our performances, but we also have to alter them and remain flexible so that we are able to adjust as the performance unfolds.

Hence in any performance, there is really a game within a game. The first game is to prepare, to concentrate, and to apply our personal performance formulas. However, the second game is to recognize, to implement, and to execute the proper combinations of adjustments so that our efforts remain directed and effective.

Let's explore some of the common issues prevalent in most types of performances.

Second Wind

Have you ever experienced the phenomenon referred to as the second wind? Most of us have been pleasantly surprised in experiencing a second wind during some kind of physical training or performing. We feel refreshed, rejuvenated, and energetic. The second wind is like a shifting of mental and physiological gears whereby the performer functions in a more relaxed and efficient manner.

The second wind phenomenon is a function of fitness and familiarity. That is, the more fit and familiar you are with your performance situations, the more mental control, physical control, and endurance you are likely to possess, enhancing your chances of experiencing second, third, and even fourth winds.

Beginners and novices rarely experience second winds for three main reasons. First, they have not yet attained the strength and endurance bases necessary for its emergence. Second, without the valuable performance experiences, beginners and novices rarely have any game plans or directions, so they become more susceptible to errors and tangents. Finally, beginners and novices are apt to have high levels of anxiety, doubt, and fear that sap their energies, take them out of their optimal performance zones, and prevent any second wind from occurring. Only through experience will beginners gain the fitness and familiarity levels needed to put them in a position to have a second wind.

Recent endorphin research seems to provide some physiological evidence for the second wind phenomenon. Reports indicate that endorphin secretions seem to be in the brain immediately preceding and during the experience of a second wind. These endorphins seem to be a natural tranquilizer, easing discomfort and promoting relaxation. Hence the performer gains a feeling of freshness and is better able to concentrate on the tasks at hand.

The second wind seems to be as much psychological as it is physiological. Through a combination of easing off and focusing, the performer can settle down into his or her most optimal performance zone. It is there that we are most receptive to a second wind. Most of us try too hard at the beginning of a performance. The start of a performance should be a time for tuning in and "testing the water." Trying softer will ease us down into our optimal performance waters. Second, third, and fourth winds are merely adjustments as the performance proceeds.

Second winds are not limited to physical endeavors. Many musicians, business people, writers, and artists have cited instances where they have gained a second wind in which they returned to their optimal performance zones even though they may have been very fatigued. Proper preparation, pacing, and concentrating all seem to be necessary to attain and sustain a second wind in any kind of performance situation.

The second wind is a performance overdrive in which the organism functions at more efficient and effective levels. All the factors that determine its emergence are still not fully known. However, what is known is that trying to bring it on or worrying about when it will emerge will surely retard it. Concentrate on your performance and enjoy your second wind when it comes along.

Mental Sticking Point

Recently, another interesting performance phenomenon has been discovered and described—the mental sticking point. This name is derived from the weight lifting term, indicating that point about midway through a lift where (especially with fatigue) the strength and position of the muscles are so weak that the weight "sticks." If this point can be passed, the lift can be completed. There seems to be a corresponding point in performances where concentration fades, energy ebbs, and resolve diminishes. These are the times when it seems easier to back off or give up entirely rather than to push on and continue.

From my surveys with various performers, I have found that this mental sticking point usually emerges somewhere beyond the halfway point (the psychological "point of no return"), but not yet to the important two-thirds to three-fourths points. At this point the end comes into view and performers can spur themselves onward. In endurance activities there may even be multiple mental sticking points that may extend as far as 90% into the activity.

Successfully passing through mental sticking points is critical because it is usually during these times that major adjustments need to be made, and the momentum must be maintained. Because the opposition may also be experiencing sticking points, the adjustments are often the critical preparatory phases for completion of the activity. If the individuals can concentrate, bear down, or simply hold on through these times, they will come to a point where they will be able to see "the light at the end of the tunnel." From there the "light" will give them the direction and impetus to effectively complete the performance.

So what can you do about your mental sticking points? First, recognize and accept their existence. As you do, you will be less apt to be affected by them when they emerge. Second, determine when and where your mental sticking points most often appear in your efforts. Also, assess specifically which forms they take in you, for this knowledge is essential to controlling them. Finally, program yourself beforehand to use these points as stimuli to spur yourself onward. Remember, your body can probably go farther than your mind believes possible. By following these guidelines, you are asserting control over your mental sticking points and redirecting their energy into springboards for maintaining or even improving your performance levels.

For example, when I am running a longer road race (e.g., a half-marathon), I know from experience that I am susceptible to mental sticking points between 7 and 9-1/2 miles into the race. So during my mental preparation, I plan to really concentrate between the 7th and 10th miles. During the actual race when I am in those miles and start feeling the temptation to slow down, I lose contact with the pack I am in, to become overly sensitive to my fatigue, or to space out, I immediately turn these around to signal the need to really concentrate and focus on my form and rhythm. I know that mentally this is the toughest part of the race for me, and if I can bear down for another couple of miles, I will be able to see the end and finish strongly.

Many labor, contractual, and diplomatic negotiations are fraught with mental sticking points. During these times impasses may become insurmountable or concessions may be made without full consideration. If the participants can endure through these periods and maintain perspective, they will be less apt to make mistakes and stay true to their positions.

Performers learning new skills often encounter mental sticking points where frustrations rise to seemingly unbearable levels. Many succumb to these frustrations and revert to older, less effective skills. However, if they can persist, the new skills will eventually become more integrated. In these instances, mental sticking points are usually indications of the last stands of the old habits. Enduring just a little longer will usually pay off.

No performance is linear. Each one has its ebbs and flows. Mental sticking points are some of these ebbs. Your challenge is to minimize and redirect these ebbs and to maximize the flows. By being aware and resisting these mental sticking points, you will not only endure, you will prevail.

Playing With Pain

Our society has fostered the crazy notion that playing with pain is necessary and even noble. Playing with pain is frequently seen as a measure of one's dedication, courage, and persistence. For me, playing while hurt is a contradiction in terms.

Remember, there is an important distinction between pain and discomfort. Pain is always physical, whereas discomfort is mainly mental. Learn to distinguish between the two. Pain is a direct signal from your body that something is going wrong, whereas discomfort is a signal that you are mentally tiring and overextending yourself.

Playing while hurt is an indication that the performers did not prioritize their energies well, monitor themselves accurately, or have enough courage to stop. Pain is honest communication from your body. Playing with pain is a dishonest abuse of your body.

With many activities and performances there is a very fine line between maximal functioning and injury. In bodybuilding one seeks to achieve a "burn," which is indicative of the inner fibers of the muscles being stimulated. However, if the bodybuilder tries to push even harder beyond this burn, chances are that a fine line will be crossed and an injury will result. Experience and awareness can tell us where these fine lines are. Regrettably, such experiences are frequently only gained from crossing over the fine lines.

Most physical performers become injured at one time or another. The important thing is what they do after they are injured. High-level performers keep in mind their long-range goals, priorities, and time lines. They also give themselves permission to adjust their goals and training instead of steadfastly holding onto inappropriate expectations. In contrast, lower level performers are less apt to remember their long-term goals and always go full steam ahead. Ironically, this "damn the torpedoes" philosophy is probably what got them injured in the first place.

Playing with pain usually exacerbates the injury, delays and prolongs the healing, and even shortens performance careers. Attempting to "run through" or "work around" an injury rarely works and may be an indication that the individual's life is out of balance. Playing with pain is not a measure of courage; it is a measure of ignorance. It takes more courage and wisdom to say no to continuing when injured than it does to acquiesce and become swept away with the moment.

Exercise physiologists are teaching us that the human body can be exercised well into the senior years. Especially with the increase in the amount of leisure time, it would be a shame to be so chronically injured that we could no longer pursue fitness and recreation. Playing with pain is one of the greatest barriers to long-term health and fitness levels.

Gutting it Out

On the surface, this section may seem to be a contradiction to the previous section. However, in many events there comes a time when, for the lack of a better phrase, one has to "gut it out." These times may occur in the 15th round of a title bout, during the fifth set of a tennis match, in the 3rd day of a training seminar, in the last 6 miles of a marathon, during the 14th hour of a rehearsal, following the third sales rejection of the day, or during extra innings of a Little League game. These are times when mental and physical resources seem to be depleted, giving up or folding looks increasingly attractive, and mental sticking points abound.

The ability to gut it out is one of the major distinctions that separates great from good performers. Elite performers prevail because they seem to have the courage, creativity, and simple tenacity to dig or reach down for something more. They seem to know how to endure or ignore the discomforts and even tap into new reservoirs of energy, resolve, and concentration.

In their own crazy ways, these times are wonderful opportunities to expand and to explore frontiers of self. I know that this may not be comforting, but those who approach such situations with eagerness rather than with dread are those who will be more able to reach down and find that almost mystical something extra. Also, those who are able to prevail in such situations will approach subsequent regular performances with the confidence summarized by the attitude, "Hey, I made it through that other event. This one will be a piece of cake!"

Be it known that the performer will pay the physical and mental prices of gutting it out. Given that reality, you must then ask yourself two questions: Are you willing to pay those prices? and Are you willing to take care of yourself afterwards?

Here are some general guidelines in approaching situations in which you may be faced with gutting it out:

1. Realize that somewhere in your performance career you will encounter such situations so that when they occur, you will not be flustered by them.

2. Remember how far you have come during this performance and convince yourself that it would be a shame to give up now. Decide that you are going to stay out there for as long as it takes. It may be grim and uncomfortable, *but it won't be nearly as bad as living with the memory that you gave up.* Even if you lose, you will at least have the comfort that you endured. Hence gutting it out can be seen as success in itself, regardless of the outcome.

3. The abilities to reach down and gut it out are dependent on your mental and physical preparation and earlier pacing, but are most dependent on honest awareness and assessments of yourself. Those who are honest with themselves are more apt to control themselves and have the courage to persist. Push yourself, but stay on the productive sides of your fine lines.

4. In competitive situations, recognize that your opponent is at least as tired as you. Use this fact to spur you on.

5. Don't be swept away with the pressures of the moment. When confronted with the temptations to try harder, reverse them and try softer. And when confronted with the temptations to slow down, reverse them and bear down. Make the necessary adjustments to stay in your optimal performance zone. This is your best insurance to endure.

6. Plan ahead and analyze after; during the effort, just go and do it!

In its own way, the human organism seems to need to push and be pushed in order to grow. Gutting it out is really a marvelous opportunity to discover just what you are made of, how far you can go, and what you can become.

Conclusions

We have touched upon some of the major themes and issues encountered in the actual performance of the dance. As with any dance, each of you in the audience is coming away with different interpretations and meaning.

What is your formula for your performance dance? What are the major components? What are the minor ones? How do you best apply your formula? Much of realizing and applying your formula is learning when it is best to analyze and break down versus when it is best to leave something alone and allow it to naturally combine with other factors.

Like any ballet, the dance of our performing is always changing, always evolving. As much as we attempt to explain and analyze our dances, there will always be enticingly missing factors. These missing factors are part of what causes performing to be such an uncertain and thrilling experience. Direct and maximize those factors of which you are aware and over which you have control, yet remain flexible enough to adapt to the demands of each performing situation. In this way, you will be creating a new dance with each performance.

Chapter 12 Performance Skills

- Most high-level performers are noted for the ease with which they execute. Their flowing movements can best be described as a dance.

- Momentum is a sign that you have brought together the mind and the body and are in your optimal performance zone. Remember, that gaining momentum and maintaining it are two separate and distinct processes.

- Although there are many forms of performance errors, they can be grouped into three broad categories: (a) errors due to poor preparation, (b) errors due to tightness, and (c) errors due to looseness. Learn the patterns of your performance errors.

- Confidence, movement intangibles, and chance intangibles are often nebulous, but they play important roles in performing. Break down each of these categories, discover the controllable components of each, and focus on executing those things over which you have control.

- There are different issues and phases during performances. Second winds, mental sticking points, and situations requiring gutting it out all occur during performances. If you are aware of these, you can use them to endure and even to extend your efforts.

- Notes: _____

  _____

  _____

  _____

  _____

  _____

- Additions or changes to your personal performance formula:

  _____

  _____

  _____

  _____

  _____

chapter 13

Go For the Platinum

All you have to do is win the last point.
—Tom Coker

When it has all been said and done, it is more fun to win than it is to lose. In any kind of an internal or external competition, winning—not losing—is the goal. Most performers go out to do the best jobs they can and hope that they will be successful. Winning is the capstone of a good performance.

Competing is a concrete barometer of achievement. After so much time has been spent on learning, practicing, and refining, competing is a refreshing change. It provides an opportunity to measure and to compare achievement. It is a proving ground to show off one's abilities. It is also a place to have fun and to learn about self.

Perspectives on Winning

Winning, scores, rankings, placings, and averages are all objective measures of performance. These measures give performers feedback so that they can continue to improve and develop. Competing and succeeding are healthy, productive, and enjoyable learning tools. Is this what most of us were raised to believe winning and competing to be? I doubt it.

Sadly, there has been so much pressure to win that most of our notions of winning, achieving, and even performing have become skewed. The pursuit of winning has become an opiate that clouds what competing and performing can and should be. In many circles winning has been constructed in such perverse ways as to be the *proof* for political ideologies, national values, religious beliefs, and even the worth of a person.

Just look at some of our everyday slogans that reflect this myopic philosophy: "Win at all costs," "Go for the gold," "Winning isn't everything, it is the only thing," "We're #1," and, of course, "The thrill of victory and the agony of defeat." How would you like to be that poor ski jumper who is doomed to go through the rest of his life being the symbol of "the agony of defeat"?

This narrow philosophy also implies that there must be losers. Look, for example, at a professional golf tournament. Using this skewed view of winning within the group of 120 golfers who tee off every Wednesday, there can only be one winner. Even if my score were one stroke behind the winner, I would still be considered a loser. So there are 119 "losers" on any given week on the pro tour. And this does not even take into account all those "losers" who failed to qualify, didn't enter, amateurs, weekend hackers, or even those who play miniature golf! But do these 119 professional golfers view themselves as losers? No way. These excellent players cannot afford to think in such narrow ways, and neither should we.

In cultures that promote such myopic views of winning, success, and mastery, the view that 99.9% can be considered losers is reinforced. This view diverts us away from what competition can be—a testing ground; a place for fun, friendship, and comraderie; an opportunity to learn how to perform under pressure; and occasions to learn about self.

If you really want to see the status of winning today, look to the children. Someday observe the Little League practice, a Pop Warner game, a gymnasitics meet, a figure skating competition, or a dance exhibition. You will see children, afraid to fail and to compete, who are miserable and who are slowly being destroyed. Worse, you will also see some crazed parents, coaches, and teachers trying to live our their outdated fantasies, modeling terrible examples of adult behavior. What do our kids think when they see such things?

The pressures to win are often so extreme and absurd that many good, wonderful, and lovely performers would rather quit than compete. Survival of the fittest, right? Wrong. When winning, success, and achievement are defined in such narrow and paranoid ways, all of us lose. Thankfully, there are other games in town. In this chapter some of the emerging perspectives on winning and achieving will be presented, along with some guidelines for balanced, consistent, and successful performances.

State of Mind

Winning is being increasingly redefined in more expansive ways. Sure, the outcome of an event is important, but so is how one performed, what was learned, and what can be applied in the future. Like most of our knowledge about performance, winning, too, is going through phases of evolution.

Although it has been used as a trite cliché by too many coaches and sportscasters, winning is being viewed with great frequency as a state of mind. As the overall meaning of winning expands, it is also becoming more diffuse, which is good. The less narrow the meaning of winning (e.g., the final score or being #1), the more able the individual becomes to concentrate on the performance at hand.

Whatever the concept means to me, if I believe I am a winner, I am. Going back to an issue explored in chapter 3, if I continually choose to build myself up, I can eventually come to the point where I can conclude that I am a winner. Regardless of the outcome of an individual performance, I can define myself as a winner simply because I have believed in myself enough to be on my side, I have resisted the temptations to be negative, I have taken the risks to compete, I have extended myself, and I have maintained my perspectives about the performance. Hence, winning—the concept as well as the outcome—becomes less crucial so that I, paradoxically, arrive at the position to perform well. True winners extend this state of mind into the rest of their lives. They seek quality and meaningful efforts in all their endeavors. They recognize that a winning lifestyle must also be a balanced lifestyle.

What defines winners is not the specific achievements or the scores but rather how they integrate and use these successes. True winners will probably be the last people to refer to themselves in such ways. This is because they have usually transcended the ego involvement that views things simply as win or lose, number 1 or number 2, a gold or silver medal, and the size of an annual contract. Winners use these achievements as indicators of their degrees of development as performers and as springboards to other quests.

The Foundation of Your Winning

What factors do you need in order to achieve the performance levels to which you aspire? I am sure you have asked yourself this question at various times throughout your life. Here is an opportunity to organize and to clarify your views about winning.

To begin, in order to find out where you are now, you must first remember where you have been. Let's start with exploring the evolution of your views and attitudes toward winning.

• What were your first recollections about winning?

_____

_____

• As a child, winning meant . . . _____

_____

• As an adolescent, winning meant . . . _____

_____

• During your younger years when you won, you usually . . .

_____

_____

• During your younger years when you lost, you usually . . .

_____

_____

Now let's assess your current views and attitudes toward winning.

- Today, winning means _____
- Losing means _____
- How have these views changed over the years?

  _____

  _____

- What did you have to sacrifice to become a winner?

  _____

  _____

- In business (or school) winning means . . .

  _____

  _____

- In your performance specialty winning means . . .

  _____

  _____

- How do you now evaluate whether you are a winner?

  _____

  _____

As we mature, our notions of winning usually take on both more expanded and specific forms. Discovering and affirming what winning and losing mean to you is a good exercise to help clarify your goals and needs and to place them in perspective. Occasionally, ask yourself these questions again to determine if your views of winning are changing.

Now let's focus on the specific qualities you need to be a winner. Figure 13.1 is a box representing the foundations from which you can build your success. Take your time and fill in all the essential components of your winning or success. I have taken the liberty of including a few of the qualities I most often hear mentioned as the cornerstones

1	5	6	2
7	8	9	10
11	12	13	14
3	15	16	4

Block 1: Quality practices, mental preparation, and physical fitness.

Block 2: A realistic positive mental attitude. A continual trust and belief in yourself.

Block 3: An ongoing state of relaxed centeredness from which effective and sustained concentration emanates.

Block 4: Experience. Both past successful experiences and the ability to learn from past negative experiences.

Block 5: _____

Block 6 _____

Block 7 _____

Block 8 _____

Block 9 _____

Block 10 _____

Block 11 _____

Block 12 _____

Block 13 _____

Block 14 _____

Block 15 _____

Block 16 _____

Figure 13.1 Foundations for building success.

of winning. Use these as jumping-off points. Feel free to change them. Now, fill in the rest of the blocks of your foundation of winning. Remember, no answer is dumb. Be honest and thorough.

This is your foundation for winning. It is your blueprint for success. Keep it, refer to it, and feel free to modify it. Remember, there are many ways of winning, and as you learn more new ways, your foundation will change accordingly. Use this information to construct your building of success, of performing well, and of winning.

Ways of Winning

A crucial question all of us have asked ourselves at one time or another is, "Just exactly how do I win?" Once when I was in the midst of along slump (no slump is short!), I went to my coach to pour out my heart about how hard I was trying and about how conscientious I was. In despair I asked, "Coach, how do you win?" Without hesitation, he responded with the phrase that headlined this chapter. Needless to say, this koan-like reply sent me for a loop. I left his office feeling angry because of his seemingly glib reply to my sincere question. But I also left his office more determined to find out the answer to my question.

If you ever have the opportunity to survey high-level performers on how they win, you will probably become as frustrated as I did when I queried my coach. At best you might receive interview-type responses such as "execution," "attitude," "preparation," or "teamwork." Most often, however, you will be met with blank looks and shrugged shoulders.

For every performer in every performing situation there are a multiplicity of possible combinations of how to win. These may include making the fewest errors, staying on course, being consistent, making the proper adjustments at the right times, proper pacing, knowing when to pounce or explode, or even stumbling into success. High-level performers may not know just exactly how they win, but they do know what aspects they need to emphasize to put them in the best position to win.

Winning and Creativity

The act of winning is a very creative process. Although high-level performers may have the same game plans, the actual unfolding of how each attains success is always unique. It almost seems that they frequently transcend the conscious aspects of themselves. Indeed, they often do. Murphy and White (1978) beautifully capsulized this point in saying,

Despite the many long years of instruction, study, practice, and training that most athletes put in, they generally do not act consciously when they make outstanding plays. The conscious knowledge of correct and incorrect moves serves as kindling and logs to a fire, but in the white heat of the event they are burnt into nonexistence, as the reality of the flame takes over— flames originating in a source beyond conscious knowledge; melding athlete, experience, and play into a single event. (p.27)

This is not to say that training and practice are useless and that all one has to do is "space out into Never-Never Land" during the event. On the contrary, training and practice provide a base from which these unique levels of creative consciousness can operate. If I am honed in on my skills, I am much more free to creatively apply them.

No matter the skill or the activity, we all go through a four stage evolution in the performing of that skill or activity. The first stage is called unconscious incompetence where we have no idea of what we are doing or even of what we should do. As we gain a little knowledge and practice, we reach the second stage called conscious incompetence. At this level we are more aware of what we should be doing but are not yet able to effectively implement these skills. As we refine our skills and develop our abilities, we eventually reach the third stage called conscious competence. At this level we are mastering and applying each individual aspect well, but we are still expending a lot of conscious energy overseeing them. As we learn to assimilate and integrate these individual parts into the whole, we reach the fourth stage called unconscious competence. At this level the individual parts flow together, and performing them becomes "second nature" to us. At this level we are free to creatively apply our skills in new ways.

In a sense, creativity is the pinnacle of much hard work mastering individual skills. At this level we can create unique ways of winning in every performance situation.

Trusting Instincts

Creatively winning is related to another important process: trust. Creative and effective performers trust their instincts and their intuitions. They trust that their bodies know what to do, and given the chance, they realize that their bodies can perform some pretty remarkable feats. As individuals better trust their abilities to perform under pressurized situations, a whole new realm of performance potential is opened for them.

Elite performers are really not as competitive as our adolescent connotations may imply in the term. Sure, they want to be successful, but they know in order to be so, they must focus their energies on themselves instead of on their opponents. They use the competitive situation to urge themselves onward but are not controlled by it; and they use the situation to channel their competitive urges inward to heighten their levels of performing.

As performers' senses of self-trust increase, they open themselves up to their instincts and intuitions. They are then in a position to almost automatically anticipate or react to various performance demands as they arise. They probably would not be able to explain it, but they instinctively or intuitively "know" the move, action, or adjustment to make. It is almost as if before they are even consciously aware of the situation, their bodies are already performing the appropriate actions.

Trust in one's abilities, skills, instincts, and intuitions is the essence of pure doing. Once in this mode the chances for winning or success are greatly enhanced.

Winning by Not Losing

Implicit in this whole discussion of the ways of winning is the necessity of making a few errors. Many contests are decided by those who make the fewest errors. Remember those performances when you "blew it" or "let victory slip through your fingers." You had success in your grasp but could not "put it away." Even at professional levels many contests are still won by not losing rather than by outright winning.

Winners know how to win, but they also know how not to lose. Being firm with their skills, controlling that which they can control, remaining sound with their concentration, and staying on course are all keys in minimizing errors and preserving success.

One mark of a great performer is being successful even when not performing well. Winning frequently means simply holding on. Remember, in many competitive situations the mind usually gives up before the body. Developing a sense of mental toughness will allow you to endure. In such situations these great performers essentially say, "It may not be an outstanding effort, *but* you're going to have to do better to beat me." Keeping your efforts fairly consistent—even if they are not up to your usual standards—will at least give you a chance for success.

Taking Advantage of Opportunities

A corollary to this principle of not losing is staying aware of opportunities and taking advantage of them when they occur. Many losses are due to either not recognizing opportunities or not knowing how to capitalize on them. Opportunities are like electric doors: They are only open for an instant and then they will shut. High-level performers use different parts of their consciousness to "sense" or "smell out" these opportunities. Once discovered they pounce on them as a cheetah does on her prey. Some call this the killer instinct, others call it adjusting to the situation. Whatever you call it, always be aware of the possibility of an opening door and be prepared to jump in.

A few years back I was interested in the killer instinct phenomenon, so I interviewed sports and business people who were renowned for possessing it. The results surprised me. Contrary to our notions about the killer instinct, most of these people were not as aggressively competitive as we might think. Sure, they wanted to win and remain a success, but they really did not focus all that much on beating the competition. Instead, they focused on themselves and on the process.

These killers concentrated on those things over which they had control and which they needed to do consistently well. By doing this they hoped to energize quickly and take the initiative in their performances. The killers were acutely aware of the progression of the performance situation. They searched for opportunities and openings to exploit, and upon finding them, they immediately rushed in and took advantage of the situation. As the end of the competition approached, the killers really bore down. This is where their mental toughness paid off in helping them see and even create opportunities. These killers were also tenacious in their abilities to gut it out; they were persistent and positive. No matter the outcome, these people knew that they had given their best efforts.

Up and down the line, the ways of winning seem to present curious paradoxes. You must emphasize your basics yet be creative. You must focus but still be able to let go. You must stay on course yet always be open to adjust. You must be sound yet be intuitive. You must be consistent but be flexible. You must pay attention yet be ever aware. You must win and you must not lose. These interplays are what make the quests for winning so elusive and frustrating yet so creative and fascinating.

Practice

How do you get to Carnegie Hall? *Practice, practice, practice.* This classic joke may be old, but it still holds true today. Planned and quality practices are another cornerstone to successful performances. We spend at least tenfold as much time practicing as we do performing, yet many performers and coaches do not know how to optimize practices.

An obvious factor that separates most high-level performers from mediocre ones is the way each views and uses practice. Most high-level performers have very specific goals for each practice. They have practice schedules and time lines that provide a sense of continuity and direction between practices. In the actual training session high-level performers concentrate only on what they need to work on. They know that quality efforts in practice will tend to carry over into quality performances.

In contrast, mediocre performers have little idea of what to work on during their practices. They tend to just "go through the motions" and are easily distracted. Some believe that they can replace quality with quantity. These kinds of practices are reflected in their performances. After disappointing results, mediocre performers learn little from their efforts and usually go back to their practices doing the same old things.

At one important level, practices can be seen as essential in promoting muscle memory. In any activity involving physical skills, purposeful and directed practices are necessary to train the particular muscles in how to efficiently execute the skill. In a way, what you are doing during these practices is educating your muscles so they can perform the skills on their own. This ties in with our old friends trust and doing. If you can trust that your muscles know how to perform an action, you can then free your mind to just doing the activity instead of having to direct every little aspect of it. Hence, practices are tools for learning how to trust your body and liberate your mind.

Quality and planned practices also enable the performer to be "in the groove." I love the images connoted by that phrase. When my physical and mental skills are honed through quality practices, my performance efforts tend to remain in a consistent groove. This groove provides the direction and boundaries within which I can perform at my best while being relatively immune to distractions and tangents. Obviously, the better my practices, the deeper the groove. I have been so ill prepared for some performances that my groove seemed like a slippery, convex sheet of ice. On the other hand, I have also been so well prepared for some performances that my groove felt like a deep valley from which any variance seemed nearly impossible.

Practice need not always be a stepping stone to performances. Practice may very well be a goal in itself. With our expanding perspectives of performing, succeeding, and winning, many people are redefining their practices more towards ends in themselves. They call this training. I know many fine runners, swimmers, dancers, skiers, bodybuilders, and bicyclists who have not competed in any event for years. They have redefined their performance goals away from external competitions in favor of personal challenges. Having as much dedication and intensity as the external competitors, they have simply retooled their goals and priorities toward more internal and developmental perspectives.

But what about those performers who want to compete? For them practices are times to dissect, analyze, think about, work on individual components, and even worry. "The trick," said Nideffer (1976), "is to learn to care and worry during practice or during breaks in the action, but to shut that out during the game" (p. 232). I know many good performers who fret and worry during practice but who bear down during the performances. It is almost as if they use their practices as releases that wash away their doubts and fears so that they can be fresh and focused during the performance.

Planned practices are also times to learn new skills and combine them with existing ones. It is essential that during these times the performers don't judge themselves or their efforts and give their minds and bodies a chance to become comfortable with the new skills. Morehouse and Gross (1977, pp. 120-125) summarized the four basic principles that must be followed in learning any new skill:

1. Be sure you have a clear image of what you are going to do.

2. Determine your starting point by seeing how far your present skills can take you.

3. Divide the skill into component parts—and start with those you can already do well.

4. Move as soon as possible to the speed of the performance.

Keeping in mind one's long-term goals is helpful in developing the patience necessary to learn new skills. It is essential to realize that it not only takes time to learn and redefine the new skill, it may also take a long time to unlearn the old, inappropriate skills. Patience, nonjudgmental attitudes, and a sense of fun in discovery are important ingredients in facilitating effective learning and integration of new skills.

Finally, practices can be used to simulate performance conditions. Especially when near a performance, practices must be directed toward combining skills and sequences in the paces and tempos of the performance situation. These practices are particularly valuable in having the performer practice concentrating. Many performers call this "putting on your game face." Simulation practices are helpful in fostering optimal levels of concentration, integration, and eagerness.

One can see that practices may take on many varied forms. It is essential for the individual performer to know when to use each form. For example, simulation practices are valuable during the couple of days before a performance, but are counterproductive when learning a new skill. On the other hand, learning a new skill is very disruptive when it is presented 2 days before a performance. Planning and specifying practices promote effective utilization of time and are the building blocks of quality performances.

Proper uses of practice, then, can be seen much like a phonograph. The grooves in the record represent the quality practices and prior performance experiences that provide the direction. The needle represents the sharp and honed mental attitudes and physical skills that rest deep in the groove. Hence, quality practices allow the individual to play beautiful music in the performance!

The Evolution of Winning

As our mental aspects of performing expand, so do our notions of winning. Winning, succeeding, achieving, and just plain performing well are taking on meanings that were unheard of 30 years ago.

Winning is evolving to mean much more than merely the final outcome: Winning is the quality of the actual performance, regardless of the final score. This evolution represents an increased coming together of the body and the mind, the means as well as the ends, rewards and responsibilities, and the integration of life roles. No longer does going for the gold seem fully appropriate. Striving for something more expanded and meaningful comes closer to the target. Going for the platinum seems to be a better representation of the quests of many of today's performers.

One of the greatest contributors to this evolving perspective of winning is from the integration of Western and Eastern philosophies. More and more performers are regularly meditating, studying Eastern texts, being exposed to Eastern orientations toward life, and synthesizing them with their own Western ideas. The forerunner of this new perspective was Herrigel's (1953) classic *Zen In The Art Of Archery*. For many Westerners this little book presented the first glimpses into the Eastern notions of performing. From this book many of us learned how even physical activities could be approached as art and as exercises of mental concentration. We learned that the mental components of any activity were much more than "psyching up" and that winning was much more than just the final outcome.

Most of us grew up believing that winning always had to be some kind of a struggle. We also believed that winning had to be equated with fierce competition. Within these views we concluded that everything was in opposition to us and was a hurdle that needed to be conquered. Our equipment, the conditions, referees, and judges, opponents, teammates, and even our bodies were the enemies that had to be defeated.

The Eastern perspectives on performing and winning presented us with a radical departure from this kill-all-opposition notion. These perspectives showed us that all of these factors could be used as allies in some greater quest. Suzuki, writing in the introduction to Herrigel (1953), posed the idea that "in the case of archery, the hitter and the hit are no longer opposing objects, but the same reality" (p. vi). Persons, goals, objects, and processes do not exist in isolated vacuums; in every performance a continuous flowing exists among them. In a sense, our minds, bodies, skills, experiences, purposes, and goals are all on the side. The key is to find the right wavelength that tunes them all together.

Think back to some of your most memorable performances. Most golfers can remember putts they just "knew" were going to go in even before they stood over the ball. The lining up, aiming, as well as the path of the ball and its dropping into the hole seemed to be one connected process. Most dancers can remember performances where very complicated steps and sequences seemed to magically flow together to create something more than the separate components. Many great baseball hitters have cited the instances in which they intuitively knew when they were going to hit a home run. The type and location of the pitch, the swing, contact with the ball, and where it landed in the stands all seemed to be a part of one long process. Many buyers and sellers have experienced times when the whole process seemed to be on "automatic pilot." Questioning, probing, and closing were transcended to a level of mutual cooperation and help.

Leonard (1978) pursued these notions further and concluded that achievement was really tied into some higher level of consciousness. Achievement was much more than just winning one isolated event. He stated, "I learned aikido from a teacher who operates from the premise that the perfect move, the perfect throw, *already exists*. Our mission was simply to join it" (p. 147). This view is quite different from the tabula rasa (blank or empty state) or the me-versus-you approaches to learning most of us have followed.

The prospects that the correct, proper, and perfect moves of a performance already exist presents more of a personal challenge to us, thus moving us away from the notions of isolation and opposition. High-level performing and winning are then more akin to joining or aligning in some kind of union. Bringing together the mind and the body, the implement and the target, the goal and the process, the hitter and the hit, and even you and your opponent in accordance with some higher existing order is winning. Joining, rather than overcoming, is viewed by an increasing number of performers as victory.

Some of these notions may sound very peculiar to those of you who have never been exposed to them before. But just sit back for a moment and remember those times when you and the bowling ball seemed to be one, and there seemed to be some kind of connection between you and the pins; or as a salesperson, you felt some kind of special rapport with your prospect, and the sales process seemed to flow in accordance with some kind of prescribed script; or as an actor or musician your part fit in perfectly with your colleagues' so that the result was spectacular; or as a wide receiver, there was some kind of intuitive communication between you and the quarterback, and you knew that you and the ball had to be united; or even in the midst of 5,000 people in a road race, you had the feeling that you were all on the same side and that cooperation replaced competition. There are some very real higher order elements to winning.

These expanded notions of winning offer much more soft, subtle, and expanded perspectives on performing. They emphasize such concepts as allowing, flowing, integrating, aligning, and trusting, instead of the old high school jock notions of forcing, opposing, isolating, and aggressively competing.

Winning is increasingly taking on more diffuse yet more personal and meaningful dimensions. Winning may mean being fit enough to enter a 10K race; it may be setting personal records for yourself; it may be meeting small but significant goals you have planned for yourself; and it may be doing things you have never done before. But perhaps most of all, winning may be proving to yourself that you can.

Chapter 13 Performance Skills

- Winning is increasingly being seen as a personal proving ground, learning center, and opportunity to extend the self. If you want to compete, fine. But realize that you do not have to compete in order to consider yourself a winner.

- Part of this new mind-set is viewing winning as a state of mind. If I truly believe I am a winner, no one disappointment is going to set me back. Much of this view is determined by living a balanced life and by keeping my successes in perspective.

- Winners know the things they need to do in order to win. They employ their personal performance formulas, make proper adjustments, and are aware of their foundations required in being consistently successful.

- There are at least as many ways of winning as there are performers and performing situations. The expanding views of winning are emphasizing creativity, trusting instincts and intuitions, not losing, and taking advantage of opportunities.

- Practice, practice, practice. There are many forms and types of practice, so learn how to use each effectively.

- Notes: _____

  _____

  _____

  _____

  _____

- Additions or changes to your personal performance formula:

  _____

  _____

  _____

  _____

c h a p t e r   14

Confluence

Whatever can be conceived and believed can be achieved.
—Napoleon Hill

I realize I have presented a tremendous amount of information in this book. Whether this information was new to you or a helpful reminder of things you already knew, the important question is, How will you remember and apply what you have read? Performing is a unique process with its own principles. Knowledge is power, and the more we know about the dynamics of our performing, the greater range we have in which to apply it.

So what are you going to do with all of this information? As with learning any new performance skill, you need to break down these large amounts of information into manageable parts, learn each part, retain it, and start putting the parts together with your established knowledge. Reread sections or chapters of this book that you haven't fully understood or assimilated. As you gain an understanding of each section, start putting it together with related sections. For example, as you better understand how to view your frontiers, put it together with your attitudes about self and specific performance goals; or as you better understand the uses of visualization, put it together with relaxation and affirmations. This coming together—this confluence—is how we integrate, synthesize, and eventually produce knowledge.

Learning psychologists tell us that depending on the information and our experience, it may take us up to 21 exposures before a bit of information is retained. So don't feel you are dumb because you have to reread portions of this book. On the contrary, those who take the time and effort to fully understand new information can better integrate it and more consistently apply it than those who gloss over it. The best way to ensure that you will retain what you have learned as you read this book is to reread, repeat, and practice. To help you, the major points of the book will be summarized in this chapter. The way I will approach this is by giving you the opportunity to chart out a performance for which you would like to peak.

Peaking

Peaking is a process by which you plan to give a maximal effort in a single performance or a series of related performances. As in climbing a mountain to reach its peak, reaching your performance peak involves many small steps that have to be well planned and organized. For the purpose of summarizing the main points of the book, write down an upcoming event in your performance specialty or business for which you would like to peak:

_____

_____

Now let's look at the major phases of the process of peaking for your performance.

Long Before

Long before the event you have to gain a clear understanding of who you are and what you want to do. A realistically positive mental attitude is a cornerstone to any success in performing. In any decision or situation you encounter, remember that you have only two options: You can either build yourself up, or you can drag yourself down. If you do not know what you are doing, you are covertly dragging yourself down. It takes more conscious awareness and energy to be positive, but in the long run, if you want to perform consistently well, you have no other choice. Always view your personal glass of water as half full.

Believe in yourself and trust that you will give your best efforts. If your performance specialty is a physical event, trust that your body knows what to do, and then give it a chance to do it. You are responsible for yourself and your actions, to assert control over that which you can control— and *always* be on your side.

Understand and face your fears, doubts, and put-downs. You will be unable to significantly improve your performances until you accept these counterproductive patterns as your own. Once you do, you are then in a position to do something about them. Actively challenge them and replace them with things you want to do. Focus on your frontiers— what you can do and be—and give yourself permission to extend yourself and to succeed.

Learn what winning and success really mean to you. Expand your views of them beyond the final outcome. As you gain more broad and balanced perspectives of success, you will also gain an increased sense of mission and purpose in your pursuits. When an event really means something to you, it will help you better connect with your drives, dedication, persistence, and goals.

Your goals and your plans to reach those goals are the specific applications of your mission and purpose. They not only give you a blueprint of your quest, but they also provide you with the initial impetus to achieve them. Keep your goals as specific as possible by making them appropriate and attainable. Reaching each little goal gives you the momentum to continue. Remember that goal setting and planning are ongoing processes, so feel free to modify and adapt them so that they remain appropriate and attainable.

As you must keep your goals specific, you must also keep them relevant to your overall training cycles. Establishing longer term training cycles provides you with the framework under which you can attain the perspectives for your individual goals.

It is very helpful to plot out your goals along a time line. Include major goals and minor ones, skill states and states of mind, as well as the dates you plan for their achievement. Plot a time line to attain your goals at the event you listed earlier on Figure 14.1. This is your performance game plan. Use it but feel free to adapt it according to how you progress. Your goals and plans are really your blueprints for success.

After you have an idea of what you are doing and where you are going, practice, prepare, and rehearse. Physically

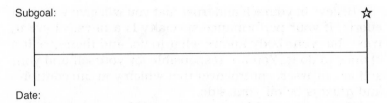

Figure 14.1 Personal time line for goal attainment.

practice and rehearse your skills and performance sequences as well as mentally prepare for how you are going to approach the performance. Be so well prepared that your efforts will almost seem to be automatic, and you can immediately react to any contingency. Prepare so well that the actual performance will be the easiest part of the whole process!

Immediately Before

Immediately before the performance spend your time relaxing, visualizing, affirming, and bringing together your skills and abilities. During this time, avoid the temptation of trying to learn anything new. Rather, focus on refining and integrating that which you already have.

Develop your own unique style of formalized relaxing and regularly use it. Relaxing not only soothes the body, it also clears the mind. View it as home base during your preparation and during the actual performance. Relaxing is pleasant in itself, and it also provides the foundation for your mental imagery and self-statements. So relax, trust yourself, and prepare.

From this foundation, learn to specifically and vividly picture just what you want to achieve and how you want to do it. Visualize yourself in the performance and actually be there. Remember, most of your mind and body cannot distinguish between something that is actually happening versus that which is being visualized. Mentally rehearse not only the accomplishment of your performance goals, but the steps by which you plan to achieve them as well. Let your images be your guides for success.

Along with your visualizations, actively talk to yourself. Affirm those skills, qualities, and attributes you possess.

Remember, trying to place positive self-statements on top of a base of negative self-statements does not work, so learn to transform your put-downs. Construct your affirmations in the present tense, starting them positively and without qualification, and frequently repeat them to yourself. Believe what you say about yourself and talk yourself into a great performance!

In the week prior to your performance, relax and taper your efforts. There is not much more you can do to add to your preparation, but by trying to do so, you will probably detract from what you have. Emphasize bringing together your skills, experiences, attitudes, and beliefs. In all parts of your life, do everything as well as you ever have. Reinforce everything you do and be optimistic. You will then be ready to perform at your best.

During

Your first goal during the actual performance is to find your optimal performing zone. In order to do this, you need to relax. Ignore distractions or temptations, and focus on the specific things you need to do. Don't try, try hard, or think. Just do. Allow your skills, experiences, rhythms, tempos, wisdoms, and instincts to naturally flow out. Be both efficient and effective in what you do. In these ways you will be able to achieve and maintain your optimal zone of performing.

From this zone you may be able to shift upwards to a maximal zone of performing. In this zone you are extending yourself farther and have the opportunity to be even more effective. However, at this level things will probably not flow as smoothly and your rhythms will be less stable. You will always have to make adjustments and attend to rapidly changing demands. Recognize that you will have to pay the physical and mental price for extending yourself into this zone, so plan for rest and recuperation after the performance. Achieving a maximal zone of performing is a risk, but so is performing itself. In doing so, you have the possibility of giving a peak performance. You are there to give your best effort so go out there and do it!

Effective concentration is essential to any good performance. Keep in mind that there are two forms of concentration: attention and awareness. Attention is placing specific emphases on certain details of your efforts, while awareness is taking in the whole picture as the performance unfolds. Learn how and when to use each form. Concentration literally means "a coming to a mutual center," so use your attention and awareness to bring your skills and abilities, mind and body, and self and situation to a concentrated center. From that center you can effectively focus and channel your mental and physical energies into a great effort.

Conserve and prioritize your energies. Early in the performance pace yourself. Control the outlay of your energies. You may be able to use the stresses and pressures of the situation to spur yourself on to greater heights. Use your mental magnifying glass to focus and to intensify your energies toward the tasks at hand. You are in charge of your performance ship, so control the energy you expend.

As you near the end of your performance, persist. There is usually discomfort in extending yourself and giving a maximal effort, so accept that and hang on. Watch out for mental sticking points. Remember, your body can usually go farther than the mind believes it can. Gut it out or simply hold on, but persist. Commit yourself to finishing with a crescendo. You will then be more apt to be proud of what you did.

After

Afterwards, rest, recuperate, and regroup. Part of the peaking process includes a recovery phase, so take full advantage of this opportunity. Extending yourself implies taking care of yourself.

This phase is a good time to objectively, fairly, and comprehensively evaluate and analyze your performance. Evaluate yourself not only in terms of the specific outcomes and goals achieved, but also in your efforts in achieving them. Sure, the results are important, but so are the means by which you attained those results. Very often, you do not have total control over the outcomes, but you do have total control over yourself in the performance process. So any beneficial evaluation of a performance should include both the means and ends.

A comprehensive performance evaluation should be viewed not as an end in itself, but as a means to further improvement. What did you do well? What would you do differently next time? How would you prepare differently? During the actual performance what do you need to emphasize more? Less? And what have you learned from this performance? About your performance specialty? About performing? About yourself? Use your evaluations as springboards to future excellence.

Compliment and reinforce what you have done during this whole process. Recognize that very few individuals have the desire, determination, and dedication to organize, control, and apply themselves. It has taken a great deal of courage, creativity, and persistence to extend yourself in this way, so pat yourself on the back and be proud of what you have done.

Use your evaluations and build upon your strengths. Based on what you have done and what you have learned, formulate new aspirations and goals. Plan and commit yourself to the goal that your next performance will be the best ever!

Performing is a cyclical process. The completion of each performance brings new challenges and objectives. Seen in this light, performing is really an ever-increasing spiral that leads to new levels of mastery, excellence, and knowledge of self.

Ends and Beginnings . . .

I hope this summary has been helpful in assisting you to better retain the material presented in this book. Use this summary as a catalyst to deeper levels of understanding, integration, and implementation of the principles of performing.

One theme I have frequently mentioned throughout this book is that there are very few ends. What might initially appear to be an end is probably a new beginning, a new means to further goals and achievements. All we have to do is recalibrate our minds to always look for these new beginnings.

In the spirits of bringing together and new beginnings, take this final time-out and fill in this assessment/goal planning exercise.

- The most important things I learned from this book are

  _____

  _____

  _____

- I am more aware of _____

  _____

- I disagreed with _____

  _____

- I did not understand _____

  _____

- I want to learn more about _____

- I want to give a higher priority to _____

  _____

- I want to apply more of _____

  _____

- My current goals for my performance specialty are

  _____

  _____

- The specific skills I want to improve are _____

  _____

  _____

- My greatest strengths are _____

  _____

- My greatest challenges are _____

- The traps I have to become more aware of are

  _____

  _____

- It is okay to _____

  _____

- I will review these assessments and goals on
  _____ (date).

. . . And Beyond

Whatever our levels of involvement and expertise, we all have the need to actualize and to maximize as much of ourselves as we can. Performing is the arena in which to show just how far we can take ourselves.

Learning, skill development, and retention are important, but so is performing those lessons and skills. Performing rounds out the total development of the person: Each dimension complements the other. Beyond that, each dimension demands the progression of the other. Performance situations—whether they be in sports, the perform ing arts, education, or business—are marvelous proving grounds not only for ourselves as performers, but for ourselves as growing individuals.

It may be hard for some of us to thnk in terms of maximums and ultimates. Leonard (1975) summarized his conception of the ultimate athlete well. It is something that can be applied to all performers and something to which we all can aspire. For him, the Ultimate Athlete is

- _one who joins body, mind, and spirit in the dance of existence;_
- _one who explores both inner and outer being;_

- *one who surpasses limitations and crosses boundaries in the process of a personal and social transformation;*

- *one who plays the larger game, the Game of Games, with full awareness, aware of life and death, and willing to accept the pain and joy that awareness brings;*

- *one who, finally best serves as model and guide on our evolutionary journey. (p. 287)*

In this day and age of increasing confluence, confusion, and conformity, we need role models more than ever. Our best models are those who have the vision to aspire, the perseverance to struggle, and the courage to achieve. And they are people just like us. They can be found on muddy running paths, in community swimming pools, in sweaty dance studios, in dark rehearsal halls, on vacant practice fields, in waiting rooms of offices, in musty corporate buildings, and in quiet rooms reading books on the psychology of performance. They are the ones who break into and explore new frontiers of themselves. They are the ones who perform at their best.

These people are you and I. Mastery, production, and even greatness are within our grasps. We just have to know how to apply and unleash ourselves. The writer Sheldon Shepard has said that demanding that greatness be turned loose within us eventually releases something greater than we are. Dare to be great—to strive for excellence in everything you do. You will never know how far you can go and what you can become until you start extending yourself.

If I could leave you with one thought, it would be the Paiute Indian saying, "In every man's life there comes a time when he must stop talking the talk and start walking the walk." It is now my time to stop talking the talk. Woman or man, young or old, athlete, performer, or business person, it is now your time to start walking the walk, discovering your own paths, and climbing your mountains.

And have a blast doing it!

Chapter 14 Performance Skills

- The hub for bringing together all this information about the psychology, dynamics, and applications of performance is the organization provided by your personal performance formula. Throughout this book I have emphasized the need for you to categorize the major elements of your high-level performances by means of a personal performance formula. It is now time to bring all of this together. Go back through the book, collect all you have written, and summarize it here. Be as detailed as you can. It will be well worth it. It is okay to include those things you need to minimize (e.g., fears, worrying, or excessive analyzing), but construct as many factors as possible in positive terms.

    Date: _____

- My personal performance formula = _____

    _____

    _____

    _____

    _____

    _____

    _____

    _____

    _____

    _____

    _____

- This can be a very meaningful thing to you. Keep it and frequently refer to it to remind you of your essentials. Feel free to modify it so that it stays a relevant and valuable tool in helping you perform at your best.

- May you enjoy chasing your stars and discovering new galaxies within yourself.

References

These are the best resources in the psychology of performance. The sources are drawn from the following areas:

* General Sports Psychology
* General Performance Psychology (including dance, business, etc.)
* Positive Mental Attitude and Motivation
* Relaxation and Visualization
* Related Psychological Foundations
* Basic Exercise Physiology

References with an asterisk following the entry are especially recommended.

References Cited

Angyal, A. (1965). *Neurosis and treatment: A holistic approach.* New York: John Wiley and Sons.

Bry, A. (1978). *Visualization.* New York: Barnes and Noble.*

Ellis, A. (1973). *Humanistic psychotherapy: The rationale-emotive approach.* New York: Julian Press.*

Gendlin, E.T. (1978). *Focusing.* New York: Everest House.*

Herrigel, E. (1953). *Zen in the art of archery.* New York: Pantheon.*

Hill, N. (1979). *The law of success.* Chicago: Success Unlimited.

Inge, W. (1957, December 16). An interview with William Inge. *Time, **70**,* 57-58.

Jacobson, E. (1932). Electrophysiology of mental activities. *American Journal of Psychology, **44**,* 677-694.

Jampolsky, G.G. (1979). *Love is letting go of fear.* Millbrae, CA: Celestial Arts.

Krause, D.R. (1980). *Peak Performance: Mental game plans for maximizing your athletic potential.* Englewood Cliffs, NJ: Prentice-Hall.

Korwin, L. (1980). *You can be good at sports.* Chicago: Sports Training Institute.*

Leonard, G. (1975). *The ultimate athlete.* New York: Viking Press.*

_____ (1978). *The silent pulse.* New York: Dutton.

Libbey, B. (1974). *O.J.* New York: Putnam.

Lichtenberger, A. (1962, Spring). Faith and fear. *Anglican Digest,* **16,** 12-18.

Maltz, M. (1969). *Psychocybernetics.* New York: Pocket Books.*

Maslow, A.H. (1968). *Toward a psychology of being.* New York: Van Nostrand.

_____ (1971). *The farther reaches of human nature.* New York: Viking Press.

McCluggage, D. (1977). *The centered skier.* New York: Warner.*

Morehouse, L.E., & Gross, L. (1977). *Maximum performance.* New York: Simon and Schuster.*

Murphy, M., & White, R. (1978). *The psychic side of sports.* Reading, MA: Addison-Wesley.*

Nicklaus, J. (1974). *Golf my way.* New York: Simon and Schuster.

Nideffer, R.M. (1976). *The inner athlete.* New York: Crowell.*

Oxendine, J.B. (1970). Emotional arousal and motor performance. *Quest,* **13,** 23-30.

Richardson, A. (1967). Mental practice: A review and discussion. *Research Quarterly,* **38,** 95-107, 267-273.

Samuels, M., & Bennett, H.Z. (1974). *Be well.* New York: Random House/Bodyworks.*

Samuels, M., & Samuels, N. (1975). *Seeing with the mind's eye.* New York: Random House/Bodyworks.

Shaw, W.A. (1940). The relationship of muscular action potentials to imaginal weight lifting. *Archives of Psychology,* **35,** 1-50.

Shealy, C.N. (1976). *90 days to self-health.* New York: Bantam Books.

Simonton, O.C., Matthews-Simonton, S., & Creighton, J. (1978). *Getting well again.* Los Angeles: J.T. Tarcher.*

Singer, R.N. (1975). *Myths and truths in sports psychology.* New York: Harper and Row.*

Vanek, M., & Cratty, B.J. (1979). *Psychology and the superior athlete.* London: MacMillan.*

Additional Resources

General Sport Psychology

Alderman, R.B. (1974). *Psychological behavior in sport.* Philadelphia: W.B. Saunders.

Bannister, R. (1955). *The four-minute mile.* New York: Dodd and Mead.

Beisser, A.R. (1967). *The madness in sports.* New York: Appleton-Century-Crofts.

Butt, D.S. (1976). *Psychology of sport.* New York: Van Nostrand Reinhold.

Cratty, B.J. (1973). *Psychology and physical activity.* Englewood Cliffs, NJ: Prentice-Hall.

_____ (1973). *Psychology in contemporary sport.* Englewood Cliffs, NJ: Prentice-Hall.

Dickinson, J. (1976). *A behavioural analysis of sport.* Princeton, NJ: Princeton Book Company.

Fisher, A.C. (1976). *Psychology of sport: Issues and insights.* Palo Alto, CA: Mayfield.

Gallwey, W.T. (1974). *The inner game of tennis.* New York: Random House.*

_____ (1976). *Inner tennis.* New York: Random House.

_____ (1979). *Inner golf.* New York: Random House.

Gallwey, W.T., & Kriegal, B. (1977). *Inner skiing.* New York: Random House.

Garfield, C.A. (1981). Mental skills for physical perfection. *Muscle and Fitness,* **42,** 47-49, 169, 172, 189, 190.

Glasser, W. (1976). *Positive addiction.* New York: Harper and Row.

Griffith, C.R. (1924). *Psychology and athletics.* Champaign, IL: University of Illinois Press.

Harman, B. with Monroe, K. (1950). *Use your head in tennis.* Port Washington, NY: Kennikat Press.

Harris, D.V. (1973). *Involvement in sport.* Philadelphia: Lea and Febiger.

Hendricks, G., & Carlson, J. (1982). *The centered athlete.* Englewood Cliffs, NJ: Prentice-Hall.

Jacklin, T. (1970). *Jacklin.* New York: Simon and Schuster.

Jerome, J. (1982). *The sweet spot in time.* New York: Avon.

Kostrubala, T. (1976). *The joy of running.* Philadelphia: Lippincott.

Llewellyn, L.H., & Blucker, J.A. (1982). *Psychology of coaching: Theory and application.* Minneapolis, MN: Burgess.

Luszki, W.A. (1971). *Psych yourself to better tennis.* Hollywood, CA: Creative Sports Books.

Morgan, W.P. (Ed.). (1970). *Contemporary issues in sport psychology.* Springfield, IL: Charles C. Thomas.

_____ (1978). The mind of the marathoner. *Psychology Today,* **11,** 38-49.

_____ (1978). The pain merchants. *Runner's World,* **13,** 64-69.

Murphy, M. (1979). *Jacob Atabet.* New York: Bantam.

Nideffer, R.M. (1981). *The ethics and practice of applied sport psychology.* Ann Arbor, MI: McNaughton Gunn.

Nieporte, T., & Sauers, D. (1968). *Mind over golf.* Garden City, NY: Doubleday.

Orlick, T. (1978). *Winning through cooperation.* Washington, D.C.: Acropolis.

_____ (1984). *In pursuit of excellence.* Champaign, IL: Human Kinetics.

Reich, L. (1974). Try not to think about it. *Runner's World,* **9**, 17.

Rohe', R. (1974). *The zen of running.* New York: Random House/Bodyworks.

Rotella, R.J., & Bunker, L.K. (1981). *Mind mastery for winning golf.* Englewood Cliffs, NJ: Prentice-Hall.

Ryan, F. (1981). *Sports and psychology.* Englewood Cliffs, NJ: Prentice-Hall.

Schaap, D. (1976). *The perfect jump.* New York: New American Library.

Schwand, W.C. (Ed). (1973). *The winning edge.* Washington, DC: AAHPER Publications.*

Sheehan, G. (1975). *Dr. Sheehan on running.* Mountain View, CA: World Publications.

Silltoe, A. (1961). *The loneliness of the long-distance runner.* London: Pan Books.

Silva, J.M. III, & Weinberg, R.S. (Eds.). (1984). *Psychological foundations of sport.* Champaign, IL: Human Kinetics.*

Simek, T.C., & O'Brien, R.M. (1981). *Total golf: A behavioral approach to lowering your score and getting more out of your game.* Garden City, NY: Doubleday.

Singer, R.N. (1972). *Coaching, athletics, and psychology.* New York: McGraw-Hill.

Spino, M. (1976). *Beyond jogging.* Millbrae, CA: Celestial Arts.

_____ (1977). *Running Home.* Milbrae, CA: Celestial Arts.

Straub, W.F. (Ed.). (1980). *Sport psychology: An analysis of athlete behavior.* Ithaca, NY: Mouvement Publications.

Suinn, R.M. (1976). Body thinking: Psychology for Olympic champs. *Psychology Today,* **10**, 38-41.

Swartz, D. with Wayne, R. (1979). How to mentally prepare for better performances. *Runner's World*, **14**, 90, 93, 95.

Thomas, V. (1970). *Science and sport.* Boston: Little and Brown.

Tilden, B. (1969). *Match play and the spin of the ball.* Port Washington, NY: Kennikat.

Tutko, T., & Burns, W. (1976). *Winning is everything and other American myths.* New York: McMillan.

Tutko, T., & Tossi, U. (1976). *Sports psyching.* Los Angeles: J.T. Tarcher. *

Ullyot, J. (1976). *Women's running.* Mountain View, CA: World Publications.

Vanek, M., & Cratty, B.J. (1979). *Psychology and the superior athlete.* London: MacMillan. *

Weber, D., & Alexander, R. (1981). *Weber on bowling.* Englewood Cliffs, NJ: Prentice-Hall.

General Performance Psychology

Burkle, R. (1971). *Nijinsky 1909.* New York: Simon and Schuster. *

Garfield, C.A., & Bennett, H.Z. (1984). *Peak performance.* Los Angeles, CA: J.P. Tarcher. *

Kriegel, R., & Harris Kriegel, M. (1984). *The C zone.* Garden City, NY: Anchor Press/Doubleday. *

Kubistant, T.M. (1984). The psychology of peaking. *Muscle & Fitness*, **45**, 111, 211, 213, 214, 216, 219.

Peters, T.J., & Waterman, R.H., Jr. (1982). *In search of excellence.* New York: Harper and Row. *

Smith, A. (1975). *Powers of the mind.* New York: Random House

Thorenson, C.E., & Mahoney, M.J. (Eds.). (1974). *Self-control: Power to the person.* Monterey, CA: Brooks/Cole.

Vincent, L.M. (1979). *Competing with the sylph*. Kansas City: Andrews and McMeel.

Waitley, D. (1980). *The winner's edge*. New York: Berkley Books.

Positive Mental Attitude and Motivation

Hammond, D.J. (1974). *The fine art of doing better*. Phoenix, AZ: American Motivational Association.*

Hill, N., & Stone, W.C. (1960). *Success through a positive mental attitude*. New York: Pocket Books.*

Murphy, M. (1972). *Golf in the kingdom*. New York: Viking.*

Peale, N.V. (1952). *The power of positive thinking*. Englewood Cliffs, NJ: Prentice-Hall.

Schwarzenegger, A., & Hull, D.K. (1977). *Arnold: The education of a bodybuilder*. New York: Simon and Schuster.*

Sheehan, G. (1978). *Running and being: The total experience*. New York: Simon and Schuster.*

Ziglar, Z. (1983). *See you at the top*. Gretna, LA: Pelican.*

Relaxation and Visualization

Kubistant, T.M. (1980). Mental imagery and performance. *Imagery, 3*, 4-5.

_____ (1982). The uses of visualization in sportsmedicine. *Sportsmedicine Digest, 4*, 6.

Richardson, A. (1969). *Mental imagery*. London: Rutledge and Kegan Paul.

Schultz, J., & Luthe, W. (1959). *Autogenic training*. New York: Grane and Stratton.*

Suinn, R.M. (1980). *Psychology in sports: Method and Application*. Minneapolis, MN: Burgess.*

Whiel, A. (1958). *Creative visualization.* New York: Greenwich Books.*

White, J., & Fadiman, J. (Eds.). (1976). *Relax.* New York: Confucian Press.*

Related Psychological Foundations

Adams, J.L. (1974). *Conceptual blockbusting.* New York: W.W. Norton.

Assagioli, R. (1965). *Psychosynthesis.* New York: Viking.*

_____ (1973). *The act of will.* Baltimore: Penguin Books.

Bosking-Lodahl, M., & Sirlin, M. (1977). The gorging purging syndrome. *Psychology Today,* **10**, 50-55.

Eisen, J., with Farley, P. (1984). *Powertalk!* New York: Cornerstone.*

Huizinga, J. (1950). *Homo ludens.* Boston: Beacon Press.

James, W. (1890). *The principles of psychology, volume 2.* New York: Dove.

_____ (1902). *The varieties of religious experience.* New York: Modern Library.

Kubistant, T.M. (1982). Bulimarexia. *Journal of College Student Personnel,* **23**, 333-339.

Spielberger, C.D. (Ed.). (1966). *Anxiety and behavior.* New York: Academic Press.

Basic Exercise Physiology

Bailey, C. (1977). *Fit or fat?* Boston: Houghton Mifflin.*

Brody, J. (1981). *Jane Brody's nutrition book.* Toronto: Bantam.

Darden, E. (1984). *High-intensity bodybuilding.* New York: Perigee.*

Hayden, N. (1977). *Everything you've always wanted to know about energy . . . but were too weak to ask.* New York: Pocket Books.

Samuels, M., & Bennett, H.Z. (1973). *The well body book.* New York: Random House/Bodyworks.

Schwartz, L.S. (1982). *Heavyhands.* Boston: Little, Brown, and Company.*

Weider, J. (1981). *Bodybuilding: The Weider approach.* Chicago: Contemporary Books.*

Index

A

Affirmations, 172, 221, 224
    activity specific, 172, 173-174
    basic, 172-173
    guidelines for using, 175-177
    process, 172, 174
Angyal, Andras, 4
Anthropomaximology, 6
Arousal, 119-121
Arousal curves, 120-121
Aspirations, 52-53
Attention, 86, 105-106, 111-112, 113, 226
Autogenic training, 126
Awareness, 105-106, 111-112, 113, 226

B

Bach, Richard, 37, 40, 137
Bannister, Roger, 14, 39
Baryshnikov, Mikhail, 14, 122
Beamon, Bob, 14
Belief, 31-33
Benny, Jack, 79
Biofeedback, 126
Bohr, Niehls, vi
Bry, Adelaide, 161
Bulimarexia, 95, 167
Burn out, 72

C

Coker, Tom, 203
Concentration, 101, 225, 226
    cocoon of, 102
    con-cen-tration, 102-103
    improving, 107-109
    scope of, 101-102
    sustaining, 109-110
Confidence, 2, 55, 188-189
Connors, Jimmy, 67

D

E

F

G

H

R

S

T

V

W

Y

Z